WARDEN

WARDEN

PRISON LIFE
AND DEATH FROM
THE INSIDE OUT

BY JIM WILLETT
AND RON ROZELLE

BRIGHT SKY PRESS

Opening photos:

Pages 2-3: Front entrance to the Walls Unit

Page 4: Jim Willett in the East Building

Pages 6-7: Upper yard, the Walls Unit

Pages 12-13: Jim Willett

BRIGHT SKY PRESS

Box 416, Albany, Texas 76430

Text copyright © 2004 by Jim Willett and Ron Rozelle

10 9 8 7 6 5 4 3 2 1

Library of Congress Cataloging-in-Publication Data

Willett, Jim, 1949–
Warden : Texas prison life and death from the inside out
by Jim Willett and Ron Rozelle.
p. cm.
ISBN 1-931721-50-5 (alk. paper)
1. Willett, Jim, 1949- 2. Prison wardens-Texas-Biography.
3. Executions and executioners-Texas. I.
Rozelle, Ron, 1952- II. Title.

HV9468.W55 2005
365'.92-dc22

2004063304

Jacket and book design by DJ Stout and
Julie Savasky, Pentagram, Austin, Texas

Printed in USA

CONTENTS

FOREWORD

BY RON ROZELLE

AFTER A CENTURY AND A HALF, IT STILL DOES EXACTLY what it was intended to do.

The Walls Unit seems to loom up forever, fortress-like. Low January clouds drift slowly over its top; whole areas of the red bricks are transformed as shadow and light play across them. The number six picket, a tiny, slope-roofed guardhouse, straddles the sharp angle of the southwest corner. The wall rises highest there, as Avenue I slopes down the western side beside the director's mansion and First Baptist Church, before the street begins its climb up the next hill to the university. A little over thirty years ago, when I first arrived as a freshman, I drove past that picket, looked up at it from my father's Chevrolet, and thought that such a high perspective must offer a fine view of the town, the university, and a good bit of the East Texas Piney Woods. Only recently have I considered what the view might be in the other direction, down into the place itself.

At the back of the unit, the road winds between the wall and a cluster of storage buildings and maintenance shops. Official vehicles are scattered around, cars, and pickups, and larger trucks. A couple of white buses sit side by side, thick steel mesh inside the windows, the Texas state seal embossed in blue on their sides.

Now the narrow road curves around the remains of a large arena, outside the walls themselves, where the prison rodeo used to be held on October Sunday afternoons. Tall brick columns rise grotesquely though much of the façade has been pried out, leaving something like the ribcage of a giant that chose this place to die and then rot. Even some of the bricks from the columns have been stripped away, revealing enough steel rebar to discourage additional tampering. Farther around, the gray grandstands come into view, steep and empty and looking down on the vast arena proper, filled now with parked cars and pickups.

The road takes another turn, and then is perfectly straight along the front of the unit. Handsome trees lift up over sidewalks, and well tended flowerbeds, and Saint Augustine grass sufficiently manicured to pass inspection in any park, anywhere. The stark, no-nonsense administration building is wedged into the exact center of the wall, a huge clock nestled underneath the peak of the steep roof. The clock could have been plucked intact out of the nineteenth century, out of Victoria Station or any number of county courthouses in the sleepiest towns in the countryside. The numerals on the clock's face are thick and black and gothic.

A small, unpretentious entrance is directly beneath the clock. A few steps lead to the single door from opposite directions. A thick, polished brass handrail gleams at the edge of the porch.

Behind those walls, inside that door, lies an area the size of two city blocks. The interior is a mystery to outsiders, some of whom grew up in its shadows. Citizens of the small town of Huntsville hear the occasional whistles; they see the lone silhouettes of restless men and slender shotguns in the pickets and on the walkways. They know that the population in there — the keepers and the kept — exceeds the population of many towns.

And they know that more people die in there at the hands of the state than in any other place in the civilized world.

■

THE TEXAN CAFÉ IS ALMOST AS MUCH OF AN INSTITUTION IN HUNTSVILLE AS THE Walls. I used to come here with other students for the chicken-fried steak and mashed potatoes. And for the pie: The glass domes behind the counter always displayed a couple of tall meringue pies, chocolate and coconut, standard fare for Texas eateries. After the meal and the dessert, we'd hunker down in one of the booths with enough coffee and cigarettes to cram for whatever exams the university had in store for us on the next morning.

Today, the inside of the place looks exactly like it did back then. Several townspeople occupy the small tables, and watch me with the lazy interest afforded to a stranger. The waitress might be the same lady who served me years ago. She makes a steady beeline from the kitchen to the tables, then back again, to bring plates of eggs and bacon and pour fresh coffee. When I tell her I'll have a cup, she collects the two dollar bills that the last diner left on the red checkered oilcloth, then holds up a menu.

"Just the coffee, thanks," I say. "I'm meeting someone."

When she's gone, I look at the two pies behind the counter. They're smaller than the ones I remember, not as fetching. They're the only things different in the room — that is, except for me and the white-haired guy at the door. He looks around till he finds me.

Jim says hello to a couple of people on the way over, shakes a couple of hands. When he shakes mine, I look hard for the boy, barely out of his teens, that I had last seen in that face. He's still there, especially when Jim says good morning. When he asks if I've been waiting long, I hear my college roommate's voice.

We spend the obligatory moments catching up. He has two kids, a boy in college and a girl in junior high. The boy is a pitcher at Panola Junior College, already signed by the Yankees. It doesn't take Jim long to tell me that; he's proud of it. My youngest girl is a high school senior; her sisters are both at Sam Houston State, over on the next hill, at our alma mater. We talk about our wives, about how we'll all have to get together. Then we talk about that tiny apartment where we lived for those two semesters, me just out of the Army and on the G. I. Bill and him already a guard. We laugh through a story or two. Then we're quiet, looking at our coffee. We each consider the reason for this reunion, weigh the pluses and minuses of a project that might be too big, too cumbersome.

"I liked your book," he tells me after a moment. "The one about your dad. Janice liked the Galveston novel, but I haven't read it yet." He grins. "Come the end of March, I'll have plenty of time to read." He'll have his thirty years in then, and he'll retire.

Four slender men come in, in leather jackets and jeans. The locals watch them, not quite satisfied they belong. The waitress is friendly, joking; she's seen them before. They say good morning to Jim. One of them shakes his hand, and they take a table toward the back.

"French film crew," Jim tells me. "Making a documentary. They've been up to the unit a couple of times. Nice guys."

I tell him I drove around the unit on my way over from my daughter's apartment. I left my wife Karen there after our two hour drive up from Lake Jackson.

"It doesn't look like it's changed any," I tell him.

The bell over the door jingles as somebody leaves. The slight clatter of knives and forks on porcelain plates blends with the sound of Saturday morning traffic on the courthouse square outside. Jim grins again.

"It never changes," he says.

A LITTLE WHILE LATER WE WALK FROM HIS CAR TO THE FRONT OF THE ADMIN-istration building. The big clock above us reads ten thirty. Jim tucks his denim shirt into his jeans and adjusts his belt, modifying his weekend clothes into something more official.

We step into a small foyer, about the size of a closet. A sliding glass window opens over a narrow counter, like the receptionist's window in a doctor's or dentist's office. There are no chairs. People presenting themselves here are expected to make up their minds quickly, and either go on in or go back out.

"Morning, Warden," says the female guard behind the window.

Jim presses his identification card flat against the glass.

"You got everything under control this morning?" he asks, sliding a clipboard along the counter. She says she guesses she does, and smiles. Jim says her name, tells her mine, and says he'll be taking me in with him.

She asks to see my driver's license. She studies the photograph, then looks closely at me. Then she asks me to print my name on the sheet.

Jim looks at his watch, and writes the exact time beside my name. He asks if anything is going on.

She shrugs. Smiles.

"Same old, same old," she says.

He nods, winks. Same old, same old is good here.

The guard calls something through the wall of heavy steel bars. A moment later a hidden mechanism clicks, a brief whirring sound commences, and the doorway opens. Jim goes through, says good morning to a couple of guards standing in the paneled hallway, and looks at framed photographs on the wall. He takes his glasses out of his pocket and puts them on.

Jim steps closer to the photos, looking for something. "One of these shows the lower yard the way it was during the death row breakout in '34," he says.

He finds it. "Look here, Ronnie," he says, tapping the frame. I start: I haven't been called Ronnie in a hell of a long time. My own sisters call me Ron now.

The photo is a black-and-white aerial shot of the entire unit. The building we're standing in was more ornate then, with a handsome façade and a clock tower. The walls were white, not yet red. Each car parked in front was an exact duplicate of the ones beside it, all of them tall, with exposed headlamps, large slender wheels, and sloping turtle hulls, spare tires mounted on the back. Where the rodeo arena now decays, the photo shows a big baseball field with covered grandstands.

Jim's already pointing to other pictures, telling me other things. He rattles off names of wardens and directors, events and dates. Architectural additions and deletions.

When he's done, he takes off his glasses and looks at me, expecting a question, a comment. Something. I lift a little notepad out of my shirt pocket and write something down. This seems to satisfy him. We turn around and go into the office across the hall.

A tall, slender fellow stands up behind one of the desks. He wears the same bluish-gray uniform as the others, but with captain's bars on his collar. He extends a big hand and says my name.

I already know Terry Green, though I've never met him in person; he wrote me a nice letter a couple of years ago after reading one of my books. We chat for a moment, and he introduces me to the guards. Then Jim and I go into his office.

Jim shuffles through memos and phone-message slips on his desk, a massive thing that takes up much of the high-ceilinged room. Tall windows look out over the front of the unit. I mumble something about there being bars even on his office windows.

"Hell, Ronnie, it's a prison," he says. He doesn't look up from the blue slip he is reading. "There's bars on all the windows."

He shows me a gift from his staff, a carved seal of the Texas Department of Criminal Justice. Shows me pictures of his children. Shows me a photograph of the office, one taken more than a half century before.

"It's the same desk," he tells me. He points to an upholstered chair under one of the windows. "That's the same chair." Where heads of corporations might be unhappy with such leftovers, he seems proud.

Back in the outer office, he asks Terry if he'd like to walk with us. Terry tells one of the guards that he'll be out for a few minutes and touches a button on the walkie-talkie on his belt. He's apparently in charge today.

In another moment I'm back out in the paneled hallway with Terry, waiting for Jim to make a telephone call from his office. Terry stands with his thumbs hooked in his belt, with the casual attitude of ease that tall, lanky people can so easily assume. He nods toward the framed photographs.

"I imagine Warden Willett showed you the pictures on your way in," he says. His voice is deep and mellow, the kind of assured, friendly voice that used to narrate Walt Disney nature films. "He's mighty fond of those pictures."

"He sure knows a lot about them," I say.

Terry's broad smile comes now, under his full, well-tended moustache.

"He ought to. He found most of 'em himself and had them framed." He searches for one in particular, a grainy black-and-white of a long, low building: "He sent off for that one from the Army archives. Cost him a little chunk of change — out of his own pocket, you understand. It was the first thing built, back before the Civil War. We'll go into its old cellblock here directly."

He continues to look at the photograph another few seconds. Then he looks at me.

"The Warden ..." he starts, but thinks better of it, and doesn't finish. He doesn't have to. Just the few minutes I've spent with this man, in this place, tells me clearly what Terry intended to say: that if I plan to write about Jim Willett, then I should make a good job of it, and tell it true.

Jim comes out now with the largest ring of keys I've ever seen. The ring itself is about a foot in diameter, and each old-fashioned skeleton key must be seven or eight inches long.

At the end of the hall, Terry calls out to a guard sitting above us, in an enclosed cubicle surrounded by steel mesh. The whirring sound commences, and a section of thick steel bars moves slowly to one side.

Terry turns to me, and delivers what must be the standard and forthright abstract of terms.

"Past this gate," he tells me, "the inmates know that there won't ever be a hostage negotiation. We don't trade, or barter. And they know it."

I nod that I understand, and we walk through the gate. It closes behind us, and the locking mechanism clicks loudly into place.

We enter a passageway flanked on either side by polished brass bars, from the floor to the high ceiling. Gleaming brass is everywhere.

"Who polishes these things?" I ask.

"Inmates that need a little extra work," Jim says. "And some of the old guys that can't do much of anything else." He touches a few bars as we walk by them. "A section or two gets polished every day."

At the end of the passage, Terry calls out again, and another gate slides away. On the other side, an open area leads to the outside yard. A large wooden podium takes up much of the space. A telephone is mounted on its side, and three or four clipboards. Several guards are leaning against the desk. They say good morning to the warden.

While Jim visits with the guards, Terry tells me this is called the searcher's desk. "It's sort of a command center," he says.

I look out into the large yard, washed with pale sunlight that has worked its way through the low clouds. The place is empty except for a few guards standing around. I ask where the prisoners are.

"In their cells," Terry says. "We're fixing to get a count."

"So they're all locked up?"

"Except for some of the trusties," He points behind me. "Like this fellow here."

I turn to see a man step over to the podium, lift a clipboard off its hook, and write something on the top page. He's in his mid-fifties. His hair is well cut and neatly combed, and something about his eyes speaks of education and confidence. Outside this place, in clothes other than a white prison uniform, he could be the accountant or dentist in the Starbucks line in front of me.

Jim rejoins us and works his way through the big keys till he finds the one he's looking for: "I thought we'd take him into the old east cellblock first. Let him get a taste of how things used to be."

He moves to a tall door, clangs the huge key into place and turns it, then pulls the door open. Air swooshes out, as if a freezer were being opened. Stepping over this threshold is like slipping from one century into another.

It's darker in here, and colder. A long hallway lies in front of us, tall windows on one side, ancient cell blocks on the other. The walls are covered with a gray, sandy material, large chunks of it gone now, revealing rough bricks set in decayed mortar. The paint on the bars outside the windows is chipped and yellowed. Every few feet, a thick pipe in its own coat of dried, crinkled paint rises from the stone floor to the high ceiling, where it turns in massive elbow joints, connecting to the webwork of pipes that encases the place like a skeleton. The ceiling, barely visible in the dimness, is covered with sheets of tin, pressed with circular designs to look like tiles. I've seen ceilings like this in old hardware and feed stores. Dust floats in the faint light from the windows and a few bare light fixtures. Even the light bulbs, larger than normal, seem from another time.

Something groans, then rumbles. The bellowing works its way along the ceiling, and its echo reverberates throughout the cavernous room. I look at Jim.

"Pressure in the water pipes," he says. "Sometimes they start knocking like somebody's taken a sledgehammer to them."

Terry smiles. "I've had old convicts tell me they had trouble sleeping after they closed this block, and moved 'em to other cells. Said they missed all this racket."

Jim pulls one of the cell doors open. It creaks. I sit down on a wide casement under one of the windows and ask when the cell was last used to house prisoners.

Jim and Terry look at each other. They've both been with the system for almost thirty years, but at the Walls for just the last few. Jim started here; he was a guard here when he and I were roommates in college. But he went on to serve in other units, working his way up through the ranks. So did Terry.

"Early nineties, I think," Jim says.

"The nineteen nineties?"

They both laugh.

"It was the most popular block," Terry says. "Inmates wanted to be in here, instead of in the newer places." He points in the general direction of the rest of the unit. "Because it was always cool in here, even in summertime."

On scorching summer days, I'd stepped into European cathedrals and felt a chill like this. Because of the thick walls, I guess. I lean against the window's casement, and some of the plaster crumbles away.

"Sandstone," Jim tells me. He reaches over my shoulder and breaks off another piece. He grinds the fragment into dust between his fingers, then brushes his hand on his jeans.

The particles fall away like pieces of time.

I TELL STUDENTS IN MY CREATIVE WRITING CLASSES THAT EVERYONE HAS A STORY worth telling. I say it often, and I believe it. Everyday life is full of drama. But I must say that Jim Willett's story is one of the best I've ever come across. His everyday life is full of sharp contrasts: life and death, freedom and imprisonment.

In this book, we've tried to recreate the texture of everyday life in the Texas prison system, not just the large events. But those large events are very much part of Jim's story. He was on hand for a prison farm riot, and for the famous Carrasco siege. He rose from a rookie guard to warden of the Walls Unit, where more men die at the hands of the state than in any other place. And there, he was called upon — eighty-nine times — to do something that he very much did not want to do.

This is Jim's story. I hope I've done a good job of it, and told it true.

JIM WILLETT AND RON ROZELLE

I HAVE NO PLEASURE IN THE
DEATH OF THE WICKED;
BUT THAT THE WICKED TURN
FROM HIS WAY AND LIVE.

EZEKIEL 33:11

EXECUTION JOURNAL

By all accounts, his was the most hideous of crimes.

I had looked through these bars into the eyes of men who'd been found guilty of deeds equally as horrible, and many looked capable of committing them. This old man didn't. He was a little short of six feet and might have been a bit heavier than the 155 pounds that his file said he weighed when he came into the system more than a decade before. His brown hair was unkempt, and he stood at the cell bars, looking out. Everything about him said that his had been a hard life, a rough one. He held a fried-egg sandwich but didn't seem interested in eating it.

I hadn't been here when the van brought him from the Terrell Unit. Usually Chaplain Jim Brazzil would introduce me to the inmate, we'd talk for a bit, and I would ask if he intended to make a statement later. We'd talk about that for a few minutes, and I'd tell him that I'd be back a little before six. This was never a surprise. They knew what six meant. Most of them had had years to think about it.

This conversation typically happened early in the afternoon, but not today. I had been to the Ellis Unit for a monthly wardens' meeting and as usual, it had run long. The Ellis warden had fed us fried catfish for lunch, and I was full and groggy when I returned to the Walls around four.

Ms. Cox had been on the bench outside my office. Her Salvation Army dress was neat and pressed; not a single silver hair was out of place. She smiled and said she was here to see Mr. Dowthitt. I told her that I hadn't yet seen him myself.

Major Katherine Cox was a constant visitor out at the Terrell Unit, as she had been for years at Ellis, when death row had been there. The petite woman would leave her Dallas-area home at one or two in the morning and drive as far as Buffalo before she pulled over at a service station to sleep for a few minutes before making the last hour of the trip. On execution days, she would often show up here because the inmate asked her to come. He's allowed a visit from a spiritual advisor, and this good woman filled that capacity many times. She also occasionally performed that final, hardest function, and watched the execution from the inmate's witness room.

In my office Tim New, my assistant warden, told me that Dennis Dowthitt, death row inmate no. 999047, had arrived at the Walls later than expected because of road construction between the Terrell Unit and Huntsville. His attorney was with him, then Ms. Cox would visit for a few minutes. Dowthitt would be allowed to make a couple of phone calls before I met him.

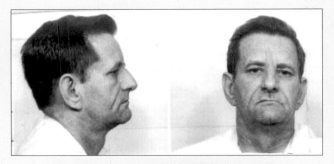

DENNIS DOWTHITT, DEATH ROW INMATE NO. 999047

His file told a horrid tale. He had been convicted of murdering a sixteen-year-old girl in June 1990. Her nine-year-old sister was also killed. Dowthitt's son Delton, then sixteen, originally confessed to both murders, but later said that his father had stabbed the older girl after raping her and told Delton to kill the younger one to eliminate any witnesses. The boy had testified against his father in exchange for a forty-five year sentence for strangling the nine-year-old.

Dowthitt looked up from his sandwich. He appeared as nervous as Warden New had told me he was. A plate of fried eggs was on the shelf beside the bunk, and a loaf of bread; he had requested a dozen eggs, over easy, for his last meal. Chaplin Brazzil told him who I was, then told him I was all right.

"I doubt you'll be able to make it through all those eggs if you eat them in sandwiches," I said.

He looked down at the sandwich again, and nodded.

"I don't think I can eat much anyway," he said. "My stomach is sorta jumpy."

I asked if he intended to make a last statement later, and he said he didn't think so. "My lawyer says there's something workin' in the courts," he said. The first glimmer of hope appeared in his sad eyes, the same one that I had seen many times in this cell.

"Well," I told him, "I'll be back out here at six, unless there's a stay."

———

There wasn't. From my office, I called our attorney in Austin and learned that the United States Supreme Court had ruled against Dowthitt. I phoned back to the death house, and asked Chaplain Brazill to tell him. Then I drove home to check on my thirteen-year-old daughter, Jordan.

Number eighty-nine
March 2001

Janice, my wife, was out of town on business, and Jordan was home by herself.

It wasn't that I was worried about her. Once, on another execution night when she was to be alone in the house, I'd lectured her about safety. "Lock the doors," I told her. "Keep the lights on. Don't go outside."

She'd stopped me. "There is an officer on a picket there, and another one there," she said, pointing to the front and back of our house. "Both have guns. Where could I be any safer?"

But I felt better after seeing her. I returned to the Walls by 5:15. A few minutes before six I put on my tie and jacket. The two calls had already come from Austin, one from the attorney general's office, the other from the governor's. Both said to proceed. I walked back to the death house.

It's a small brick building, tucked in the northeast corner of the walls under the number one picket. It consists of eight cells, plus the execution chamber, its adjoining IV room, and two witness galleries. Most of the time, the whole place is empty.

Dowthitt was sitting on the bunk. Chaplain Brazill was just outside the cell.

I said the inmate's name, and recited the line I'd delivered eighty-eight times before: "It's time to go with me into the next room."

He didn't need subduing. He didn't even hesitate. He walked with me toward the green door at the end of the cellblock.

Where the electric chair used to be now stands a sheeted gurney. It takes up most of the small chamber, a hard room made of brick walls, tiled floor, and cold steel. I told Dowthitt to lie down on the gurney. Five men known as the tie-down team came in and fastened thick leather straps over his arms and legs. The longest strap crossed his chest.

While the crew did its job, I stepped out into the block and asked if I could borrow someone's watch. Mine was in the shop, and I needed one. After the lethal injection was completed, I always allowed three minutes to pass before I asked the doctor to make his examination. A fellow from the regional director's office loaned me his. I slipped it on, and Mickey Mouse looked up from its face. Not the best of choices, given the circumstances, but there was nothing to be done about it.

Back in the chamber, the tie-down crew waited for me to inspect their work. I pulled lightly on the straps and asked Dowthitt if any were uncomfortably tight. He said they weren't.

"Well," I said, "are they loose enough for you to try to escape?"

He made a half-hearted attempt at a grin. "No," he said, "but if you loosen 'em a little, I might try."

I thanked the tie-down team and dismissed them. The medical team came in to insert the IV. While they went about their work, Chaplain Brazill unfolded the sheet and placed it neatly over Dowthitt's lower body. I was standing close to the inmate now; he looked up at me.

"I never was able to eat them eggs," he said. "My stomach was too jittery." He glanced toward the chaplain. He waited a moment before going on. "We had us a long talk. About my boy." He looked then toward the window to his right, where he knew the witnesses would soon be standing. "And...everything."

A member of the medical team had already inserted the IV in one arm, and was now dabbing alcohol on the other one. Dowthitt squealed, and the man jumped. Dowthitt chuckled.

"Most folks wait till the needle goes in to do that," the attendant said.

"I forgot to do it the first time," Dowthitt said. "I guess it was a delayed reaction."

The medical team left, and there were just the three of us in the little room. Dowthitt lay still under the straps and looked for a long moment at the speckled tiles of the low ceiling.

"Chaplain," he said, "I want to thank you for spending this afternoon with me." He nodded in Brazill's direction. "You're a fine man."

Brazill placed his hand on Dowthitt's knee and squeezed lightly. His hand would stay there, I knew. He always did that, to let the inmate know that he was there.

I asked if he had changed his mind about making a final statement.

"I think I will," he said. "I want to say a word or two to my sister."

In a moment, the witnesses were led into the galleries on the other side of the window. Not wanting to intrude, I hardly ever glanced over there, but I did this time. The woman in the victim's witness section was undoubtedly the murdered girls' mother. She stood just a couple of feet from me, as close to the glass as she could get. Her stern gaze was focused intently on Dowthitt. She had waited more than ten years for this, I supposed. Her daughters would have been grown up by now. They might have already given her grandchildren.

When all the witnesses — inmate's, victims', and media — were in place, the deputy director of the Texas

Department of Criminal Justice stepped out the door of the IV room and told me I could proceed.

It was time for me to ask if there was a last statement. Then I realized that Dowthitt's last name had slipped away from me. I searched for it frantically, but my mind wouldn't send it out. I could recall only his first name.

"Dennis," I mumbled, hoping no one would notice, "you may make a statement now if you wish."

He looked first at the black microphone suspended over his head, then toward the girls' family. He told them he was sorry for their loss. Just that. I had heard a good many confessions in this room, but this didn't sound like one. He began to sob.

"If I was y'all," he told them, "I would have killed me."

Then he turned toward his sister. He told her he loved her, said he had to go, and asked God to bless her.

Dowthitt looked at the girls' family again, at their mother.

"Gracie was beautiful, and Tiffany was beautiful. You had some lovely girls, and I am sorry." The sobbing had become something more frantic now; he had to pause for a few seconds. "I don't know what to say."

He looked up at me now, and caught his breath.

"All right, Warden," he said, "let's do it."

For a long time, I'd lifted my glasses from my nose to signal the executioner, watching through the one-way mirror, that it was time to begin. But that signal had been described on a radio documentary, and a condemned convict had heard it and mentioned it to me on his final afternoon. So I came up with a new plan. From Radio Shack I bought an inexpensive two-piece alert device. I put one piece in the executioner's room, and the other I kept in my pocket. I kept my hand in that pocket. When the time came, I pushed the gadget's button, and a tiny light went on in the other room.

The executioner then started the first of three infusions through the IV line. Sodium thiopental, which puts the inmate to sleep, is the same stuff used in operating rooms countless times every day. Then he administered a muscle relaxant to deflate the lungs and diaphragm. Finally he started a massive dose of potassium chloride to stop the heart. When he was finished, the executioner switched off a tiny light attached to the overhead light fixture — a signal to me.

Three minutes later, Mickey's huge hands told me it was time to call the doctor. I shielded the watch's face from the witnesses and noted the time of death for the record.

Less than an hour later, when the funeral home had removed the body, and the witnesses and media had gone, I stepped out the front door of the Walls. I was tired, and

I felt the same gnawing in my gut that came with each of these. I knew that I would sit down at my computer later that night or early the next morning and write about the day's proceedings. Journal entry number eighty-nine.

I couldn't get Dowthitt's statement out of my thoughts. Or that bit about his visit with the chaplain. About his boy. Without a doubt, both father and son were guilty of a horrible sexual crime. But I couldn't help wondering whether the boy had killed both girls and handed over his old man in exchange for a lesser sentence.

Jordan was home by herself, and I was anxious to be there.

Home.

Where my family was safe. Where things made sense.

Dennis Dowthitt's was my last execution. The two others scheduled before my retirement were stayed.

During the two weeks leading up to my last day, I became a minor media sensation. My picture appeared in all the big Texas newspapers, along with interviews and articles. *The New York Times* ran a front-page story. Photographers and reporters spent a lot of time with me.

But they were gone on the last day, and I was glad. I spent the day answering congratulatory phone calls, going out to lunch with the ladies who worked in my outer office, and packing up. Around seven, I was done.

I looked around the office, and was surprised there wasn't a bigger lump in my throat. It wasn't really my office any longer. The huge pictures of my son and daughter had been removed from the wall behind the desk. All the personal things were gone. It was just a room now.

I took one last look around and turned out the lights. I picked up a phone in one of the outer offices and called the captain's office.

"This is Willett," I said. "This is my last call. I'm on my way out the door."

On the front porch, I watched the first stars trying to make themselves known in the evening sky. There was a slight breeze in the East Texas air, and a hint of the piney woods in the night. Tomorrow would be April; tomorrow I would be retired.

A final thought came as I slung my jacket over my shoulder and lifted out my car keys. I never had an inmate escape while I was a senior warden. Not a single one.

But eighty-nine had gone into a small room with me. And none of them had come out alive.

001

THE METAL STAIRWAY WAS STEEP, THE NEW UNIFORM was stiff, and the muggy East Texas night was intense. But not as intense as the unsettled stomach and nervous headache I was carrying to the small guard tower, the number one picket.

The man delivering me, an Officer Black, trudged up the narrow steps. People who worked in the prison system, I was learning, were addressed by a title in front of a last name: Officer Such-and-Such, Warden So-and-So, Mr. Whats-His-Name. Only prisoners lacked titles, and no one seemed to have a first name.

The guard in the tower had lowered a key on a rope, and Officer Black unlocked a metal door encased in the same red bricks that seemed to cover everything there. I fell in behind him on the caged stairwell, and was already sweating in the rigid new garb.

We climbed up through the trapdoor under the watchtower into the small room. Officer Black introduced me to the man I was relieving. We shook hands, then the two men counted the ammunition while I looked around. The upper portions of all four walls were windows, opened as wide as they would go to let in any breeze that might miraculously wander that way. A tall, straight-backed chair stood by one of the two doors that opened unto the catwalk. There was a small heater, a toilet, and no sign of an air conditioner. The fellow going off duty left Officer Black watched him go down the stairs, hoisted the key back up on its string, and watched the guy walk off into the night. Then he turned his attention to me.

"It's all pretty simple," he said. "Call in every hour on the hour."

He pointed to a phone. It was glossy black, sharp at its bulky edges, and looked heavy enough to serve as a boat anchor. It was a twin of the one at my dad's office, in the Pearl Beer warehouse in Mexia, except that this one had no dial.

"Whoever's at the searcher's desk answers it when you pick up the receiver."

Officer Black pointed to the cord that hung from the overhead light, a bare bulb screwed into a porcelain base. He tapped the cord and made it dance.

"Flash your light every half hour. Then the number two picket will flash, and all the way around to number eight." He moved his hand in a slow, wide circle, following the direction the flashing lights would travel. "Then the number eight picket will call the searcher's desk to let 'em know the flashes got all the way around."

He grinned. Winked. "That's one way we make sure you fellows are all awake. And alert."

I didn't figure I'd have trouble staying awake. I was more than a little nervous about the prospect — however remote — that I might have to shoot somebody.

We stepped out on the narrow catwalk that wrapped around the tower. A few gnats buzzed in the still summer night. A locomotive groaned a lament. A dog barked.

The number one picket was perched on the northeast corner of the Walls, directly over the warden's residence on the outside, and the small death house inside. Because of a Supreme Court ruling, there hadn't been an execution in Texas or anywhere else in the United States since 1964. So the little building sat locked up, dark and unused in the most remote corner of the unit. The officer who had given me my tour the day before had pointed in its general direction, then moved on to what he considered more important places.

Officer Black leaned down and rested his arms on the guardrail. "You can't see much from here," he said. "Except what you're supposed to be lookin' at." He nodded at the well-lit tops of the walls.

"There's the chapel," he said and pointed to its steeple, reflecting smudges of moonlight. The slanted roofs of several buildings — all of which looked as old

THE EAST BUILDING, THE OLDEST PRISON BUILDING IN TEXAS

as any structure in Texas — were covered with red Spanish tiles. The sides of the buildings were made of the same red bricks as the walls that encased them.

During my tour, I'd heard that the East Building was the oldest prison building in Texas, and one of the oldest in the South. It had been built somewhere around the middle of the nineteenth century, and some of its cells housed northern prisoners during the Civil War. I had stood in the cramped little solitary confinement cubicle — smaller than most closets — where the outlaw John Wesley Hardin spent more time than he did in his cell.

I had never before been in a prison. I was surprised how neat and orderly everything was. There was fresh paint on everything that could be painted, and a high shine on everything that could be shined. The floors, be they tile or concrete, shone like countertops.

I was as nervous as hell on that tour, walking through hundreds of convicts in white uniforms. The captain waded through them, unfazed, but I could see them watching me, maybe sizing me up. I tried not to make eye contact with any of them. A buddy who was a guard had told me that real prisons weren't anything like the ones depicted in movies, but I still carried old, deep images that didn't match the shining floors. I had first heard of prisons back in Groesbeck when I was a boy. Charles, a kid my age, lived up the road from our place, and his daddy got sent to the pen for stealing cattle. Charles never talked about it, but adults said that it was a hard place, full of long days of backbreaking work, with no family or house to go home to. I knew then that I never wanted to be sent to a prison, and until now, I'd never considered working in one.

The tall, steep roof line of the administration building blocked any view of the number eight picket on the northwest corner. I was familiar with the administration building, and though I couldn't see the clock faces high under the apexes of its roof, I knew they were there. One clock faced out to the free world and gave the residents of Huntsville a constant opportunity to set their watches. The other one faced into the upper yard of the prison, and reminded its inhabitants of that one thing that they had perpetually on their minds and on their hands. To the south, the façade of the long building in the exact center of the unit rose up. It separated the lower yard from the upper, and I'd heard that when it was built the prisoners dubbed its close confinement block the Shamrock, after the fancy hotel in Houston. Beyond it, the huge workshops of the lower

THE NUMBER ONE PICKET

yard — the license plate plant, print shop, box factory, boiler house, mechanical shop — sat empty.

Officer Black asked where I was from.

Groesbeck, I told him.

He smiled. Rubbed his chin. "The Goats," he said.

I grinned; I'd played for the Goats. "How do you know that?" I asked him.

He told me he was from Marlin, less than thirty miles from Groesbeck, on the same rolling grasslands of central Texas. We talked for a few minutes. Then he said he had better get back to his duties. I watched him go down the stairs, his short, stocky body taking each step carefully. I liked him. He wasn't afraid to smile, and I figured I had found at least one man on the place that I could ask about things.

When he was out of sight, I went back into the picket and took a quick and careful inventory of essential things. There was the thirty-eight-caliber pistol. The twelve-gauge shotgun. The telephone. The toilet.

INSIDE THE NUMBER ONE PICKET

I sat down on the tall chair and commenced watching for inmates attempting to escape, then offered a pretty good prayer that they wouldn't choose that night to do it. I looked at my watch, so I wouldn't be late for either my call-in on the hour or my one quick flash of the overhead light on the half-hour. The congregation of buzzing gnats was the only indication that anything was going on anywhere. Even that dog hadn't barked in a while.

The gothic spires of Old Main, the most impressive building at Sam Houston State, were bathed in a soft floodlight on a hill to the south. I was a business major, and had taken a couple of classes in Old Main. As a freshman, I'd spent too much time partying and not enough paying attention to my classes; only a heart murmur had kept me out of Vietnam. But now I was becoming more serious about my grades and the future. Someday I wanted to work in an office, at a desk.

Until the day before I'd worked at a gas station in town, but the pay was low and I had a hard time scheduling the work around my classes. A friend recommended that I try the prison system, which at first wasn't encouraging. A sign at the personnel office said that more than three hundred people had applied for positions throughout the system. I called the personnel officer repeatedly, hoping to improve my odds. Finally, worn down, he told me to come in for an interview.

He talked to me for a while, asked a few questions, and had me fill out some forms. Then he asked when I wanted to start work. The pay was good, almost five hundred a month, with a raise of a little over thirty dollars after six months if I stayed. That was almost double what I was making at the gas station.

I told him I needed to give a day's notice to my boss at the station.

Mr. Allen wasn't surprised. It was a college town, and countless gas jockeys had wandered through his station. He asked where I'd be working, and I told him. He puffed on his pipe a couple of times, then sent out a long, slow line of smoke.

"Jim," he had said, looking me square in the eyes, "you'll never make it there."

I asked why.

"You don't have the personality for that kind of work. You won't like it."

I told him I was going to try it, thanked him for the job, and finished my day.

And so here I was. The time came for me to flick the overhead light on and off, to signal the number two picket that I was awake and alive and paying attention. I watched as the guard there flashed his light twice, and flashes worked their way around the top of the tall brick walls. I looked around the inside of the picket again, for probably the fiftieth time, to make sure everything was where I thought it was. The shotgun. The pistol. The phone. The toilet.

I stepped out onto the catwalk into a night that had grown even warmer. I leaned on the rail, looked into the darkness, and wondered what I had gotten myself into. If I kept this job, there would be a lot of this gazing off into nothing. I had never suspected that pure and simple boredom could be a job hazard. But, I reasoned, boredom was a damned sight better than something happening. At least in this place.

002

THE SMALL TURN-OUT ROOM WAS FULL OF PEOPLE awake earlier than they wanted to be. The older men were feeling their age. The young ones had stayed up too late driving around or drinking at The Risin' Sun or Randy's Rec. Or, less likely, they'd been studying for their classes.

The men were yawning, making sure that buttons were buttoned and shirts were tucked in, and rubbing eyes that wanted to be closed. From out of the cold morning, we'd all come into this room that was almost as cold. Everybody still wore his jacket. Nearly everybody was smoking. Chairs scraped along the floor, and the place clattered with slow and uninspired activity.

I yawned, and scrunched tighter in my gray uniform jacket. I still occupied the lowest rung of a ladder that I didn't understand or even especially want to be on. I was a rookie, a "new boot." I didn't know many of these guys, so I'd have hesitated to enter a conversation even if any had been taking place. But everybody just smoked, and yawned, and tried to rub a little warmth into his hands.

The first shift always started in here, with the yawning and coughing and smoke. After six months of climbing into a picket at nine-thirty and watching the old prison and the old town sleep away the night, I had been assigned to the first shift. It was a welcome change. I was tired of working while my college buddies partied, and I had determined that, for a while longer at least, I could shuffle the hours at work with my classes. The extra money meant more beer, more albums, more dates, and my first new car, a Toyota Celica that my father, ever the World War II veteran, disliked because it was Japanese.

At last Lieutenant Cauthen came in, looked over the group, and fished two squares of paper from the pocket of his uniform jacket. Without a greeting, a nod, or any other acknowledgment that there were other people in the room, he began to read the morning's IOCs — interoffice communications — word-for-word from the top.

"To all staff. From Warden Harvey. Effective immediately, when bringing food or other items into the unit, these guidelines will be followed. Containers must be not greater than one gallon in capacity and must be made of a see-through material. There will be no exceptions."

Cauthen took a long pull from a can of Tab — he was never far from a can of Tab — looked at the square of paper for a minute, then put it in his pocket and looked at the other one. In his mid-fifties, he was just a few years shy of his retirement. Age and the beginnings of a beer belly caused him to move slowly through his duties, the primary of which was to send younger men off to theirs. He smoked one cigarette after another. Coming from his smoker's throat, the IOCs and duty assignments sounded like tires on a gravel road.

"To all employees," he growled. "From Warden Harvey. Effective immediately, when an inmate is given solitary confinement as punishment in his disciplinary hearing, the inmate will be taken directly to the infirmary for medical clearance prior to being placed in solitary. There will be no exceptions."

Every IOC started with "effective immediately" and ended with "there will be no exceptions." I wondered why the phrases weren't printed on the forms.

Cauthen lifted a clipboard and read out duty assignments for the day. I huddled a little tighter in my jacket, rubbed my palms against my knees, and hoped to draw a shift inside one of the cellblocks, where it would be warm. Or maybe I'd land an ambulance run over to the Huntsville hospital with a sick prisoner. Or even better, a Galveston run, escorting a convict sick enough to require the prison wing at John Sealey Hospital. I'd spend the better part of a shift in a heated vehicle.

Cauthen barked names and assignments, drank some Tab, and said the word that I dreaded.

"Utility."

Utility officers performed jobs that didn't require an entire shift. They worked the chow line, or shook down the inmates arriving on a bus, or escorted prisoners to any of a hundred places in the unit.

"Willett," he barked. Two other names followed. "Go catch the end of the chow line."

The short walk between the main building and the inmate dining room was cold enough to make the three of us hope for inside jobs all day. It wouldn't happen, of course, and we knew it. But hope is free, and it runs in abundance in prisons.

The business of preparing, serving, and eating breakfast was already in full operation when we stepped into the inmate dining hall. The big room echoed the clank and clatter of silverware against metal trays. Clouds of steam rose off coffee in more than a hundred cups and from the table pitchers that convict waiters kept filled. The yeasty aroma of hot biscuits mixed with that of fried sausage. The tall windows were fogged against the north wind.

INMATE CHOW HALL

WARDEN

I said good morning to the guard I was relieving and watched him zip his jacket and go out the single door. Everybody, guards and inmates, wore jackets, and though it was considerably warmer than outside, the winter morning found its way in through the door, which was constantly being opened, and through too many old vents in too many old walls. The best place to be was in the center of the room. And the worst place was near the door, where the chow line snaked in from the ramp.

That was where I had to be.

Working the chow line was boring, with nothing much to do but make sure the convicts got in the right line, which they always did without prompting. They could sit anywhere they wanted, but they always sat in the same places: whites and Hispanics in the north side of the room, blacks in the south side. The serving lines were in the middle. All I had to do was make sure that nobody cut in the line or swapped food, and that everyone ate everything he took.

The wind whistled along the steep ramp on the other side of the door, and some of that wind blew in with the men in line. A few nodded at me as they went past. Some said good morning. Most just went by as if I weren't there. I didn't even need to tell them to speed it up this morning. Not with that draft pushing them up the ramp, like geese ahead of a blue norther.

I was glad I didn't have to bark orders. I had been raised to show respect to my elders, and practically every inmate on the place fell into that category. Most were old enough to be my father; some were old enough to be my grandfather. I still hadn't worked out the tricky balance of giving orders and showing respect. These were the bad guys; I knew that. Some had committed crimes so horrible I could barely imagine them. And some, I knew, would kill without thinking if it would deliver them back into the world. Nobody had told me that — for some reason I hadn't been sent to the short training course for new boots — but I knew instinctively what convicts were capable of, given the opportunity.

Those grim possibilities seemed remote, though, on a bone-chilling morning when the convicts weren't doing anything more sinister than eating sausage and eggs. They sat in groups of four, on stainless-steel stools that were welded to the table. They leaned over their trays and focused their attention on their food. They were allowed to talk quietly, but only to the other three men at that table. Not much talking went on. When each man was finished with his meal, he balled one hand into a fist and knocked once on the surface of the table. Then he unfolded himself from the metal stool, lifted his tray and his cup, and walked away. Nobody knew where the knocking had begun, or why. And, like most rituals, it was carried on devoutly without any need for such explanations.

One old convict walked past me to return his tray. There were two biscuits still on it.

"Hold up there," I told him. He stopped.

"Go back over there and finish eating those biscuits."

He contorted his old face into a pained expression. "Can't take 'em, boss," he said. He rubbed his stomach. "Full."

The rule was that you eat what you take, and he knew it. He wouldn't have wasted his breath on an older officer. I nodded in the direction of his table. He went back and sat down.

I looked up and down the line. Told a few men who had stopped to talk to move it along. Listened to the sporadic knocking of fists on the tables, like the uneven pumping of a huge heart trying to find its rhythm.

Lieutenant Cauthen came in and looked around. He popped open a fresh can of Tab, and walked over to me.

"Catch the pill line when it comes time," he said. The other two guards working the chow line grinned, happy not to be me.

When breakfast was over, I walked past the table where the old convict had been sitting. One of the large metal water pitchers sat where his tray had been. Two biscuits floated in there — bloated bonus points on a scoreboard.

Me versus them. Two points for them.

003

CLOUDS THE COLOR OF COLD STEEL HUNG HEAVILY
over the upper yard, low enough to look like a blanket
draped over the walls. I had the whole wide place to
myself as I walked quickly across. The wind scraped
along the ground.

I knew that it was at least this cold home in
Groesbeck, less than a hundred miles to the north. I
thought about my parents' warm house, two blocks
from the Baptist church and just up the road from the
Limestone County courthouse. Daddy would already
be gone, hunched over the steering wheel of his Pearl
Beer truck, tapping the heater to coax out more
warmth. Mother would need to leave for work soon,
too — in Mexia, she managed a dress factory — but
right now, she'd be cleaning the kitchen after breakfast,
wiping down the counters and the tabletop where the
two of them had just eaten buttery scrambled eggs,
biscuits, and sausage or ham. The television would
be on in the living room, but Mother wouldn't be
watching or even listening. It would just be on, maybe
as evidence that the world continued to function on
such a bleak morning.

Outside the hospital, I waited for Charlie to open
his pill window. A long line of regulars already stood
in the maze of metal handrails that led to the window.
Of the roughly eighteen hundred prisoners at the
Walls, at least a hundred would stand in the pill line

WILLETT ON RAMP

on even the worst of days. Like this one.

I watched the men shiver in their white jackets, and wondered, not for the first time, at the logic of distributing medication outdoors. It stood to reason that an inmate sick enough to need medicine was likely to become even sicker after standing in cold, wet weather. But I wasn't anywhere near the level of importance to make suggestions or ask questions, so I just waited for Charlie to open the window.

Finally he did, and as the inmates handed him their scripts — prescriptions from the prison doctor — he dispensed their pills, along with paper cones filled with water. After each inmate received his pill, he had to face me, so I could watch him swallow it and throw the paper cone in the garbage. If the inmates were allowed to walk away, many would save their pills until they had enough to get high, or they'd trade them to other inmates for something more important than their health.

Charlie wasn't breaking speed records this morning. Of course, he was inside the warm pharmacy with a heater at his feet. I never minded the job on hot days, since, at the Walls, you were apt to be hot wherever you were. But today the north wind whistled around the corner of the hospital with a vengeance, and

I could think of any number of better places to be. My ears were numb, and my hands. I hated cold weather, always had.

Just when I thought things couldn't get worse, Old Man Smith presented himself at the window. He'd been locked up in the Walls forever, and nobody, officer or inmate, liked him. His eyebrows scrunched low over his mean eyes, his forehead crisscrossed with as many lines as a city map. He wore, as always, a go-to-hell smirk.

He put his script on the counter, then flicked it toward Charlie with one spindly finger. Charlie looked up, mumbled, shook his head. Old Man Smith smiled, satisfied that he had pissed somebody off.

Charlie gave him his pills, a whole handful of them. Smith stood and looked at them for a long moment, then rolled them around in his palm. Getting them just right, I guess, before he threw them into his sorry old mouth. More likely, he just wanted to make me wait. Me and the convicts shivering behind him.

He nearly dropped one, saved it, then recommenced rolling the pills around.

"Come on Smith," I said. "Take the damn pills and get out of here."

He looked at me. Smiled the little screw-you smile that he had perfected. Finally, he jerked his cupped hand up to his mouth, tossed in the lot, and swigged water from the paper cone. He took his time, bobbing his head up and down to get the pills down his throat. When the performance was done, he crumpled the cone, dropped it in the can, and turned to leave.

"Whoa," I told him. "Hold 'em up and show me."

Now he turned and gave me the dumb, innocent look, like I was the problem here.

He waited, delivering his line with an actor's sense of timing.

"I'm jus' doin' what you tol' me, Boss." Each word, each facial expression, was sharpened to insolent precision. "I'm gettin' out of here."

The wind sang out around us. The convicts behind Smith hunched their shoulders and shuffled their feet against it. My ears felt like ice cubes.

"Open your mouth," I told him.

He nodded. Dropped his lower lip slightly, then clamped it back into place.

"Open your damn mouth and move your tongue around like you're supposed to. You've been through this a thousand times."

He did it. Slowly. Overemphasizing every movement.

"That all?" he asked.

"It will be as soon as you open up those hands."

He looked put out now, like it was his patience that was being tested. Then he smiled, and spread his hands wide. They were empty.

Our eyes locked for a few seconds, then he emitted a low smirk of a laugh.

"Get the hell out of here," I told him. He turned and sauntered off toward his cellblock.

The twenty or so inmates in the line watched him go. Then they looked at me.

The old bastard would be warm in his cell before I was through with this duty. My father would be unloading cases of Pearl Beer at a country store, or maybe having a cup of coffee with the owner. My mother would be driving to Mexia, tapping her fingers on the steering wheel to whatever tune the radio was sending out.

And I would still be standing in this cold yard, wishing for spring. Wishing for graduation. Wishing for a future away from walls and smart-assed old men.

004

THE WHITE PRISON BUS RATTLED INTO THE SALLYPORT under the number four picket, belching sooty exhaust fumes into the bitter gray morning. Its old brakes squealed a protest as it stopped just short of the fence. The gate closed behind it, and it was trapped.

It was barely an hour short of noon, but the dismal day hadn't yet improved. Beside the sallyport, the columns of the old rodeo arena rose through the wispy winter fog, the tops almost lost in the low clouds. Thin skeletons of utility poles reached up, the nearest ones sharp and precise, the ones further away like lines tentatively drawn with soft charcoal on damp parchment. The steel bars and links of the fence were chilled like implements in meat lockers. The north wind still swept down from the arctic. Past Canada, past northern states where someone might expect it to be this cold, past Groesbeck, past the ornate clock on the administration building. Past the long number four and five buildings, and into this small cubicle of steel and mesh, and a bus full of reluctant men.

Those of us standing beside the bus weren't looking forward to the procedure, either.

Every weekday morning, buses arrived from all over the prison system. And on days when I was a utility officer, about half of my shift was spent shaking down the inmates who climbed off those buses, recording any property that they would be allowed to keep, and relieving them of any that was forbidden. Just about everything was forbidden.

Almost all of these convicts were just passing through, to stay overnight in the transient block until they went to another unit the next day or were discharged or paroled. All those transients made it a royal pain to get a precise population count at the Walls. Most prisons are filled with inmates who don't ever go anywhere. Those places do what prisons were designed to do: keep people locked up. But at the Walls, hundreds of inmates went in and out on any given weekday. Every one of them had to be accounted for, every minute of the day. That accounting is nothing like the cash box at a drug store. There, if there's a dollar less than the cash register receipts show should be there at the end of the day, it's no big deal. But if one prisoner is missing, then all operations come to a grinding halt until the stray is located.

So things went slow, and everybody took their time — especially in the sallyports and the shakedown rooms, with the incoming men. Even the offloading of each bus, secure in its cage, was a drawn-out affair. And on a frigid morning like this one, it seemed even more drawn-out than usual.

The bus driver handed a packet of paperwork out to the sergeant. It was a thick bundle, full of all the travel cards, medical records, and other files that convicts never got to touch, but which always accompanied them on their odyssey of incarceration.

The inmates, handcuffed together in pairs, stepped down in their white uniforms. They huffed against the cold, and moved in single file toward a holding pen. Some gave a brief, obscene appraisal of the weather, as if registering a grievance against something we controlled. The four-letter words became small white clouds of vapor that quickly dissipated into the hazy morning. One old man stepped heavily down, then farted with the vigor of a bay mule. No one — not even the convict directly behind him — protested. The men were probably glad he had waited till he was off the bus.

The sergeant checked each inmate against the mug shot on his travel card, then handed the cards to me. The old convict shifted his weight from one foot to the other for a moment, then stepped forward. I looked at his card.

He'd been in for thirty years this time, all of it down at the Darrington farm. Before that he'd served a couple of short stretches at other units. A typical story: His two brief forays back to freedom had provided just enough time and opportunity

THE EAST GATE

to land him back in, the second time with sufficient consequence to get him a straight thirty. Now he was being paroled.

I often flipped through the old men's cards, just to see where they had been and how long they had been in. It wasn't uncommon to see an inmate number that consisted of only five digits, which meant that old boy had been in for a hell of a long time. Some had been in longer than I had been alive, some much longer. I read on one old convict's card that he had been given lashes, long ago, for violating a rule. A veteran sergeant told me that, until the '40s, lashing had been a common punishment, administered with "the bat," a long, leather strap with a handle.

When everyone was accounted for, we moved the men into a holding pen, then took the fortunate half into the shakedown room. The other half had to stay outside in the enclosure, like cows in a feedlot.

Inside, I took my place behind one of the tables; the convicts all stripped down to their prison-issue boxer shorts and stood in a cluster to wait their turns.

Working in the shakedown room was torture in summer. The convicts had ridden, sometimes for long distances, on an un-air-conditioned bus. On hot days, the crowded place stank like the locker room I remembered from my years as a Groesbeck Goat — except that the stench was worse, as if real goats were involved. It wasn't unusual for two hundred men a day to pass through that room. Tempers were short, the humidity was high, and the inmates were surly.

It was better on cold days, when two gas heaters, one at each end of the room, ran at full force. But shakedown was still one of the worst duties to pull in the Walls.

I pointed to the old man, and he moved slowly up to my table. The card said he was sixty, but I would have guessed seventy, or even older. He leaned forward slightly, as if his frame was tired from supporting even the slight mass of wrinkles and flab that it carried.

"Going home?" I said.

He exhaled. He smelled like cigarettes; most of them did.

"Gettin' out," he said. We both knew where his home was; any other was probably long lost to time and circumstance. Chances were good that he would see this room again.

Every inmate in the Texas prison system, from whatever unit, was delivered back into the outside world through the front door of the Walls, the same door that I had first entered when I hired on. This old fellow would step out that door in a day or so. Probably nobody would be out there waiting for him, so he would likely walk down the hill to the bus station and take another ride — not on a white bus this time — to wherever he intended to get on with his life. He would have to contact his parole officer there, and get himself some sort of a job.

I always hoped they wouldn't come back. It wasn't because of numbers; we would always have buses full of men to process and a prison full of men to contain. But I liked to hope that the ex-cons would make a go of it in the free world. Even this man, old and bent, with putrid skin the color of the clouds and fog outside, could still have something of a life outside.

"Empty the contents of your travel bag out on the table," I told him.

I'd discard things they couldn't keep — things that bent the rules, like a fan without a guard, and out-and-out contraband, like a small motor that had been modified into a tattoo gun.

He didn't have anything like that. I looked at his stuff: a cheap Zippo lighter; a package of coffee; a plastic mug that might have once been white; a package of cigarette papers and state-issued RJR tobacco (it stood for R. J. Reynolds; the convicts all called it Run Johnny Run); two Milky Way bars; a tube of ointment; a toothbrush and a bottle of state-issued tooth powder. Inmates were allowed to keep ten letters, and some of our most memorable outbursts came when they had to choose which ten. But this fellow only had one. It was so old it was starting to turn yellow, and the careful handwriting on the envelope was beginning to fade. Only one letter in thirty years? I wondered. Or just one that he cared to keep? I checked off each item on a three-by-five card, took the first of many deep breaths that I would take that day, and moved on to the next part.

"Take off your shorts," I told him.

He lifted one spindly leg out, then the other, and stood before me in all his sagging glory

"Open up and move your tongue around," I said. The pill line had given me plenty of practice for this particular sequence.

Then I asked him to stretch his hands out wide and turn them over. I told him to show me the soles of his feet.

"I gotta lean on this wall to do that," he told me. I nodded.

Even against the wall he had trouble keeping his balance, but he managed to lift each sole high enough for me to see that nothing was taped there. He landed heavily back down and grimaced a little, either from the small jolt to his skeleton or in anticipation of what we both knew was next.

This was unquestionably the single worst part of my job.

"Bend over there," I said, "and spread your cheeks."

He leaned over as far as he could, but had to keep one hand on the wall. He used the other hand to stretch first one flaccid half of his ass out wide, and then the other. It was my task, of course, to make sure that nothing was concealed in his rectum. I remembered the force with which he'd farted, and considered it unlikely that any contraband could have remained intact. But I looked anyway. There was nothing there, other than the obvious reason for his tube of ointment.

The next man at my table was young enough to be the old man's grandson. I didn't know what crime he had committed, but if it was robbery, the proceeds must have gone to a tattoo artist. He must have had thirty tattoos, everything from naked women — a whole harem's worth — to a large cross emblazoned "JESUS." He emptied the contents of his bag and nodded as if he were proud of the

INSIDE THE SALLYPORT

collection. He had his ten letters, each addressed in different handwriting. There were a few toiletry items, including shampoo, conditioner, and three different brands of hair gel. And most significantly, he had a book about legal rights and a couple of court documents.

Most convicts spent much of their time inside trying to get back out. I would have, too. The inmate writ-writers in each block were kept busy all the time, and some prisoners put together little mountains of paperwork. A few weeks earlier, a bus full of convicts had pulled into the sallyport with a white prison-system pickup right behind it. The bed of the truck was filled with one inmate's legal paperwork. We had him unload the papers and take them to the bull ring, a large room used as a holding area. We sorted them on a long table. The inmate commanded us to be careful of his paperwork, and not to read any of it. "I have my rights," he kept telling us. We felt sure he knew them all.

The tattooed man watched as I riffled through his possessions. He was about my own age, and the muscles in his chest and arms were evidence that he made frequent use of the weights at his previous unit. I hadn't looked through his card, so I didn't know if he was being paroled. But I doubted it. He had the cocky look of a kid in for a long stretch. He'd probably got crossways with somebody at his unit and was being reassigned to another one. He'd spend one night at the Walls, then move out on another bus in the morning.

I picked up one of the letters, and he showed the first sign of interest in what I was doing. By the time I got to the fourth or fifth envelope, the naked girl on his left forearm was performing a nervous little dance.

I tilted the envelope, and a single photograph spilled onto the table. A plump, pink girl of eighteen or nineteen filled most of the frame. She had twisted her ample frame into a spread-eagle pornographic pose, thrusting her gaping cavity toward the camera. It seemed at home here in a room where other cavities stood gaping all day long.

I picked up the photo.

"We'll be destroying this," I said.

His eyebrows knitted down into an angry look for a few seconds. Then he slipped quickly into a lackadaisical sneer. I don't care, it said. Who gives a damn?

But I couldn't move on to the next part, the visual search of this human canvas of artistic delights, without knowing something.

"Is that your girlfriend?" I asked.

He laughed with enough enthusiasm to set a dozen tattooed scenes into motion. "That ain't no girlfriend of mine," he said. "I wouldn't have no girlfriend that would do such as that and let somebody take a picture of it."

I looked at the photo one last time.

"Then who is this girl?"

He didn't laugh this time, but smiled — a wide, knowing smile that said more than any tattoo could convey. A beaming smile that said here is a guy who has the world figured out. "That there's another convict's girlfriend," he told me. Then the smile grew, amazingly, even broader. "I give him half a carton of Winstons for it."

005

WHOEVER POUNDED ON MY DOOR THE FIRST TIME DID it again.

"Willett," he shouted, "phone call!" He gave it one more wallop, hard, to drive the point home. The disadvantage of having a room near the front of the BOQ — bachelor officers quarters — was that you had to answer the only phone in the building, and then go fetch whoever the call was for. The guys in the other three bunks groaned. Pulled pillows over their heads. Mumbled some things. I crawled out from under the prison-issue blanket, got my bearings, and lumbered down the hall.

On the previous afternoon, Sergeant Ed Trainor and I had taken our Little League team to Houston to watch the Astros play in the Dome. Our team had just completed the first undefeated season for twelve-year-olds in Huntsville's history, so Ed and I figured the boys deserved an outing to a major-league game. It had gone seventeen innings, and by the time we had driven seventy miles back to Huntsville, dropped off the kids at the Little League park, and listened to parents carp about the wait, I hadn't fallen into bed until almost two.

Now it was four. Ed was on the line, as alert as if he'd had a full night's sleep.

"Willett," he said, too loud and too briskly, "they got a problem out at Ferguson. I'm at the warden's office. He says for you to get your uniform on and get over here. We're going out there with him."

I grunted a few words, went back to my room and got dressed. Then I walked, yawning, across the street to the Walls. To the officers in the six and seven pickets, I must have looked like a drunk staggering home.

This was Ed's doing, of course. When the warden had called him to go to Ferguson, Ed had probably suggested that I come too. The warden liked Ed. So did I. His lean, tall body didn't set him apart from many men who worked in the Walls, but there was something about him that inspired confidence. When he found out I liked baseball, he'd asked me to help him coach that team. I'd slowed my college schedule down to a couple of courses a semester by then, so I had the time. And I'd moved into the BOQ to cut expenses. Baseball practice — like any opportunity to get out of the BOQ — was welcome.

WHEN I CLIMBED THE STEPS ON THE FRONT PORCH, I HADN'T EMERGED FAR enough out of my grogginess to be concerned about — much less fear — the prospect of going in the wee hours of the morning to a prison that had a "problem."

But I was fully awake and sufficiently frightened a little while later, as Warden Harvey sailed his big car around the twists and turns of the narrow farm-to-market road that traversed the nearly twenty miles of pasture land and forests out to the Ferguson farm.

Ed sat in the front with the Warden. Nobody said anything. At least I didn't hear either of them doing any talking up there. All I kept hearing, over and over in my mind, was the single word that had been used several times in the warden's office.

Riot.

A short word, but one that packed the effectiveness of a cold shower and a gallon of coffee.

I was fully awake.

WE MADE OUR WAY QUICKLY THROUGH THE GATE AND THE FRONT OF THE UNIT. Warden Harvey started sniffing.

"They used tear gas," he said.

We came to a corridor between cellblocks. It was full of people. Someone handed me a gas mask and told me how to use it. By the time I got it strapped on, my eyes were burning, and tears puddled inside the rubber seal. I could taste the gas, even more so when I swallowed. In a few minutes it got better.

Dr. George Beto paced the long hallway like an angry man waiting, not too patiently, for something that should have already happened. His narrow-brimmed fedora, as natural a part of him as his hands, glided above his handsome pressed suit. He held his own mask at his side, and seemed unaffected by the fumes. Maybe he was naturally immune, or maybe his constant movement lessened the effect. Probably he was so focused on the riot that his attention was not about to be diverted by anything as inconsequential as tear gas.

He was the Director of the Texas Department of Corrections, and he was old, at least from my vantage point. Everybody called him "Walking George," owing to his habit of showing up at the prisons in his system at any hour of the day or night and walking briskly through to see how things were being done. He was a stern man, with a stern demeanor but he had been known to break into a quick smile. This morning was not a smiling occasion.

I blinked my eyes inside the mask, and tried to find a level pattern of breathing — which was difficult, given the lingering taste of gas, the close confines of the mask, and the anticipation of what might happen next. After several months of a daily routine — of working the chow and pill lines and checking feet and assholes in shakedowns — I had settled into boredom. But now things were likely to change.

The riot had begun the night before. It started about rack-up time, around ten thirty, in a cellblock of black inmates. Then it spread throughout the entire unit. The convicts destroyed television sets, benches, and almost everything not bolted down. They threw their work boots out onto the runs and into the hallway. Warden Kenny Coleman ordered the tear gas to be used, and the cellblock quieted. But now the question was whether the inmates would buck instead of going to their jobs. A convict "bucks" when he refuses to do something he is told. If one inmate bucks, it's a problem. If a bunch buck, it's a sit-down. If they harm somebody, or destroy something, it's a riot.

In my short career, I had never seen any bucking at all. I had always assumed it went on — I had seen as many prison movies as the next guy — but this would

be my first encounter with it. If it happened. And I sure as hell hoped it wouldn't.

Dr. Beto kept to his pacing, stopping only occasionally to receive a report or give an order, holding his gas mask the way a woman might hold a purse that she didn't really need and wished she hadn't brought.

MIDMORNING, WE WERE TOLD TO GO OUTSIDE AND LOAD UP INTO VANS AND THE backs of pickups. In a few minutes we headed out to the fields, a thick cloud of dust billowing around us as we bounced along the bumpy road. I held tight to the lip of the side of the truck. Ed sat beside me. He didn't appear concerned about where we were going or what we would do when we got there. So I tried not to be, either. But it didn't work.

The little convoy pulled to a stop at the edge of an enormous cornfield. Fifty or so of us climbed out, and a Ferguson officer started passing out hoe handles and short lengths of rope.

"They're bucking," he told us. He said it in a way that indicated that he, for one, wasn't a bit surprised. It was the sixth day of July, and his gray uniform was drenched at the armpits and at the collar. Hundreds of inmates were sitting on the ground out in the vast cornfield, like so many large white birds among the green plants. These were younger inmates than the population at the Walls, and they were stronger both because of their age and the hard work they did on the farm. The whole group was surrounded by highriders, guards on horseback armed with rifles, who sat and watched and waited. The officer handed me a hoe handle, which I turned and hefted like a baseball bat. It seemed a better weapon than a piece of rope.

I was about to tell Ed this when another officer ran up to the first and told him something. The first officer made a face to show that he wasn't surprised by this, either.

"Dr. Beto says we can't use the hoe handles," he spat out. "Give 'em back."

All of the sections of rope had been distributed. I was left with nothing in the way of defense.

A brilliant summer sky spread out over the potential battlefield. The open field sweltered in the humid late morning. It was good to be out of the gas mask,

AERIAL VIEW OF THE FERGUSON UNIT

but now I could feel cool sweat beginning to collect on my neck and my forehead. I squinted in the bright sunlight and looked at the prisoners. A few looked back at me. Come on, their attitude seemed to say. Come on.

I wondered what the hell this job had gotten me into. I had moved substantially further away from Groesbeck and that gas station job than I had ever intended. But here was a thing that had to be done, and I was expected to do it, even if it turned into a bloody business. If there was blood, I was sure that not all of it would come from prisoners.

We moved out as a group, slowly advancing toward the field. I stayed close to Ed, and just put one foot in front of the other one. When we were almost to the first of them, the convicts finally stood up and started slow-bucking — doing some work, but at the rate of cold molasses being poured. We stopped, and watched them for a few minutes, all of us pleased that we wouldn't have to advance any further with the ropes. Or, in my case, without one. Then the wagons came. The inmates loaded up and returned to the unit for lunch.

Ed and I were sent to the black slab, a concrete area between the main building and the back gate, where inmates turned out for work in the fields.

Somebody brought us johnny sacks — the prison term for meals served in paper bags — and we waited for the convicts. The question now, of course, was whether they would go back into the fields.

"They won't let 'em slow buck this time," Ed said, his lean jaw wide with a bite of his sandwich. "They'll have to work regular." He chewed a minute. Thought. Looked over at me. "We might have to make 'em work. This time."

I nodded. I was tired and sleepy, and my eyes still hurt from the tear gas. And I had rarely wanted anything as badly as I wanted a foot or so of rope.

Finally the rear door of the main building opened, and the inmates moved out. Slowly. Straggling. Slow-bucking. I figured we were in for it.

All of a sudden, Major Dick Andrews bolted out the door behind them, moving as fast as his rock-solid, stocky body could go. He wore his red hair in a perpetually short, sharp crewcut, and his face, this afternoon, was as red as his hair. He looked like a little allotment of pure hellfire.

"Get your asses out that back gate!" he yelled. "*Now!*"

Ed and another officer on the slab started running toward the convicts. They were swinging the short lengths of rope over their heads, so I swung my arms in the air as if I had one, too. The inmates moved out quickly and headed for their jobs.

We followed them to the fields, where they went to work and didn't buck. We stood under the blistering East Texas sun and watched them all afternoon, until they were loaded up and returned to the unit. Then Warden Harvey told Ed and me we were going home. The words were sweet. I had roughly enough energy left to make it back to our vehicle.

The warden and Ed talked most of the way back to Huntsville, and I dozed for a minute or two while pastures and pine trees and houses slid by. Out the window, I saw a young guy sitting on the steps of his front porch. He watched his kids running around in the front yard. I watched them too, until they disappeared from sight. Then I watched the countryside until we rolled into Huntsville. As we drove down Avenue I, the Walls rose up beside us.

Ed looked back and asked if I was okay.

I nodded.

I'd been to a riot now, and I damned sure didn't want to go to another one. I wanted to put this job behind me, and graduate from college, and get on with my life. And never again need a short piece of rope.

EXECUTION JOURNAL

It is small and windowless and constructed of red bricks made by prisoners. Two locked cyclone-fence gates and a narrow sidewalk separate it from the day-to-day activity of the rest of the penitentiary. On average, it is used once or twice a month, usually on a Tuesday or Wednesday afternoon. Today is a Wednesday.

Inside are eight cells and a walkway in front of them. There's a table in the walkway with a small arrangement of artificial flowers — not the good kind that look like real flowers, but the obviously plastic ones. The display is the lone attempt at something bright or festive in a place where any such endeavor is doomed to fail. A single green door, no wider or narrower than any ordinary door, leads to the small execution chamber and its adjacent rooms, one for the executioner and two for the witnesses, victim's and inmate's, divided by a single thin wall. The whole place is smaller than your average dentist's office.

Joseph Cannon, death row inmate no. 634, is locked in his cell. Until this afternoon, he was at the Ellis Unit, where death row has been housed for years. Once Texas dispatched condemned men to the hereafter at a much speedier rate, and these eight cells accommodated the enterprise nicely. But the Supreme Court's halt of capital punishment in the early sixties and a lengthy appeals process created a surplus of prisoners on the row, and new digs had to be found. So now, usually early in the afternoon, a white prison van brings the inmate scheduled to die. He is kept in a cell, usually this one, until six o'clock. Then he either walks or is manhandled down the short walkway and into the last room that he'll ever have any business in.

It's about one thirty now, and the newly arrived inmate has a long afternoon in front of him. He can receive a visit from his lawyer if he or she made the trip to Huntsville for the event; and a visit from his spiritual advisor if he has one. Chaplain Brazzil, as usual, will spend most if not all of the afternoon with Cannon. He will be allowed to make a few phone calls, and at four they'll bring his last meal from the kitchen. He placed his order sometime last week out at Ellis: fried chicken, barbecued ribs, a baked potato, salad with Italian dressing, chocolate cake, chocolate ice cream, and a chocolate shake.

But before any of that — before the lawyer, or the chaplain, or the food — he gets a visit from me, the brand-new senior warden who hasn't even officially taken over yet. Morris Jones, the man I am replacing, has clearly had enough of this particular aspect of the job, and pushed this one execution to the new guy. I don't blame him. I wish I could give it to somebody else myself.

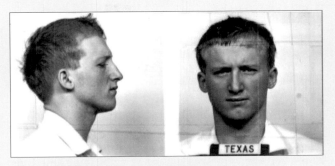

JOSEPH CANNON, DEATH ROW INMATE NO. 634

So here Cannon and I are, looking at each other through steel bars. I've been in the prison system for twenty-seven years, and will retire when that number becomes thirty. This is the part that I've always dreaded, the one aspect of a complex job — like one narrow pigeon-hole in a massive rolltop desk — that I had hoped to avoid. And here is Joseph Cannon, who has been in the same system, in a different capacity, for almost as long: twenty years on death row. He would just as soon skip our six o'clock appointment, too.

This morning I spent time with his file. The kid who looked back at me from his first prison photograph, taken when he was nineteen, was lean and handsome. Two years before that photo, he had been tried in San Antonio for some unimpressive crime. His court-appointed attorney, Dan Carabin, had gotten him off, and Carabin's sister — Anne Walsh, another San Antonio lawyer — had taken sufficient interest in the teenager to let him live in her house while he served his probation. One day in September 1977, Mrs. Walsh came home for lunch and was promptly shot seven times with her own .22-caliber pistol. Cannon attempted to sexually assault her body, stole some cash and two fifty-dollar traveler's checks from her purse, took several more guns from the gun rack, and made his getaway in his victim's daughter's car.

A few hours later, he was pulled over and arrested. He made a full confession before the officers could get him to the police station.

He's thirty-eight now and bears little resemblance to the teenager in the photograph in his file. He's bigger and wears the tired, worn-down look that many prisoners acquire. As I talk to him, he nods a little and glances toward the green door.

"You'll be getting your supper after awhile," I tell him. "And the chaplain will be here with you until...."

Now my eyes dart toward the door.

Hell, I'm not very good at this. I've worried about it for a couple of days. I know that I need to get some sort of a sense of how he'll behave later, when we're in there. I've tried to think of ways to make him feel at ease, at least as much as possible. Looking toward that door is most definitely not the best way to do it.

"Will you want to make a final statement?" I ask.

He thinks. Nods. "I guess I will."

We mumble through other items of business. Like when I'll know that he is finished with his statement. And when the witnesses will be brought into the rooms on the other side of the glass. Chaplain Brazzill helps us through it. Of the three of us, he's the only one with any experience.

▬

It's a little after five. I can hear new voices in the outer office. One belongs to Wayne Scott, an old friend who went to work as a guard at the Walls a couple of months after I did. Now he's the big boss, the Director of the Texas Department of Criminal Justice. He stands in the doorway, wearing a suit that probably cost more than his first month's salary back in 1971.

Following him into my new office are Wayne's boss, the chairman of the State Board of Criminal Justice, and my immediate boss, the regional director. Janie Cockrell, one of the deputy directors, is with them. It's my time in the spotlight.

A few minutes before six, we're all in the death house when the two telephone calls come in. One from Governor Bush's office, the other from the attorney general. Both say to go ahead. Wayne looks at me. So does the chairman. So does the regional director.

I walk down to the second-to-last cell, where the chaplain is waiting with the inmate. I nod at Cannon, and he nods back. As if we're agreeing that we've got this little thing to do.

"Inmate Cannon," I say, "It's time for you to go into the next room with me."

He does, without resistance or any need for encouragement. He stops in the door for just a couple of seconds and looks at the gurney. It takes up most of the small room, and is covered with white sheets. I don't even have to tell him to get up on it.

The tie-down crew does its job quickly and leaves.

Two people from the medical team come in to attach the IVs. A third member — formerly the executioner's assistant — is in the next room and will serve as executioner. One employee has been the executioner for almost the entire time that Texas has been administering lethal injections, but he's been ill lately, and his assistant has taken his place. Rookies abound.

One of the medical technicians begins her search for a vein in each arm — one for the introduction of the fluids, the other for a backup. Warden Jones told me that even on a bad night, inserting the IVs will take maybe ten minutes.

Almost a half hour later, the technician is still poking around. Finally she looks up at me: "Warden, I think we've got a good one on this one arm. Can we go with just the one?"

I nod. During the time that it took her to locate this one, good vein, Cannon has been quiet on the gurney. Chaplain Brazill made a few attempts at small talk. Cannon sort of smiled once or twice, and either shook his head or nodded at something that Brazzill said. But he didn't talk and watched as the technician jabbed at one place and then another. He's got a hell of a lot on his mind right now, I imagine. And all that chocolate may have made him nauseous.

When the vein was located, he bobbed his head slightly. Probably he was glad that the puncturing was over.

Now only three of us remain in the room: Cannon, the chaplain, and me. The prison higher-ups and the medical team have stepped into the executioner's room. A local doctor waits in the cellblock.

Cannon looks down at the IV in his arm. Looks at the black microphone above his head. He turns his head to the side, and looks at the plate glass window beside him. He watches the witnesses as they move slowly into the two small areas on the other side of the glass, like water filling a tank. One woman, on the inmate's side of the partition, stops in her tracks when she sees him strapped to the gurney. She stands there for a minute, then somebody behind her puts a hand on her shoulder. She moves closer to the glass.

Cannon watches her. His face doesn't indicate regret, sorrow, or a plea for forgiveness or understanding. Maybe the lack of expression is a mask to cover all those things. Or maybe he doesn't feel them at all. The woman is probably his mother.

The viewing areas are filled. Five members of the victim's family are allowed to come, and five people that the inmate chooses. The two groups are always kept separate the entire time that they are in the unit. They stay in different waiting areas, and are led to the death house at different times. The closest they come to each other while here is at this moment, with only a thin wall between them.

Five members of the media are allowed, and Warden Jones told me they usually huddle beforehand and make sure that reporters are in both rooms in case something interesting or newsworthy happens. Jones told me the Associated Press guy from Houston is here every time, and somebody from the Huntsville Item, and Wayne Sorge of KSAM, the local radio station. Usually there's a reporter or two from a paper or television station where the crime took place.

All the witnesses stand, looking through the glass like a maternity-ward crowd on a busy day.

Janie Cockrell, the deputy director, steps out of the executioner's room.

"Warden," she says, with a sufficient gravity in her voice to underscore the drama of the evening, "you may proceed."

I take a short step closer to the gurney.

"Inmate Cannon," I say, "you may make a statement at this time if you care to."

He mumbles a few things. He's nervous, of course, and the IV ordeal certainly didn't help. He rambles, talking about his family, his crime, his victim. All of it is jumbled together. At the end of it, he shakes his head and closes his eyes, no doubt having said very little that he intended to say.

He's quiet. And waiting. Chaplain Brazzil stands near his feet; he rests his hand on Cannon's ankle. I reach up and lift my reading glasses away from my nose — the signal for the hidden executioner to start the first of the fluids flowing. We're all waiting. I am overwhelmed, fully aware of the weight of the signal I've just given. I notice that it's quieter than a place with twenty-five or so people so closely congregated should be. It's quiet enough to hear the solution moving though the IV line.

"Warden."

Unsure who spoke, I look at the chaplain.

"Warden," Cannon says again. "It fell out." He moves his eyes in the direction of his arm.

This problem with the needle is called a blowout, and I was told that it hardly ever happens. I can't see it from where I am, so I shift a bit. And there is the needle, lying beside his arm, spilling its contents.

I tug the curtain to shield the witnesses, but it doesn't budge. When I pull harder, the fabric comes unhooked at the top. Chaplain Brazzil, on the end with the drawstring, has better luck, and manages to cover the glass. Someone, probably Cannon's mother, is crying. I step to the door and tell the staff to remove the witnesses. The medical team does its work a little more quickly this time, and the IV is secure. The witnesses are led back in. The curtain is opened.

We begin again. I ask Cannon if he wants to make another statement. He does better this time. He looks directly at the daughter of his victim and tells her he s sorry.

I give the signal. Joseph John Cannon goes to sleep, then draws his last, loud breath. Three minutes later — the longest three minutes that I have ever spent — I ask the doctor to come in. He pronounces the inmate dead at 7:28 p.m. — about an hour later than I had hoped.

Later, after the witnesses are gone and the Huntsville Funeral Home has removed the body, Wayne Scott and the chairman of the Board of Corrections shake my hand and say goodnight. They don't say "good job."

I know that I'll never want to do this. But I can hope that my next execution, and all the ones that will follow, will go better.

█▄▄█

The house is quiet when I get home. Jordan is in her room, doing homework and talking on the telephone. Janice sits across the dining room table and watches me move food with my fork. I stare through the window into the night.

Soon we'll move into the warden's residence, which is located just outside the walls, not far from the number one picket, which hovers over the death house. The place where I will eat with my family, where I will joke with my kids and watch mindless TV shows with my wife, lies about fifty feet from the little room where I take off my glasses and shut down a human life.

Entire continents could fit in that space.

006

THE SEVEN INMATES WATCHED AS I SEARCHED FOR THE right key on the ring. Their hands were stuffed deep in the pockets of their white jackets, and though it was a nippy morning, they weren't anxious for me to locate the key and open the door. They had all been back here before. It would be colder inside than out and — more importantly — they just didn't want to go inside the death house.

The small cellblock and even smaller set of rooms attached to it were cleaned every week. They never got very dirty, since they were never used, but Texas prisons employ the philosophy that if something can be cleaned or polished or painted, it should be. Idleness is frowned upon — the devil's workshop and all that — and with endless free manpower at hand, no job inside a penitentiary ever needs to be left undone.

So every Tuesday morning, somebody brought a crew of convicts to give this place a good going over. This morning it was me.

The prisoners followed me in, then each one instinctively moved to the left, down to the cells. Away from the closed door on the right. Away from the thing that they all knew stood just behind it.

I called out five names, and told those convicts to dust the bars and the bunks. To sweep and mop. To get the place in pristine shape so it could sit for another week, useless and cold and dark. A musty,

stagnant ambiance had long since settled on the rooms, and no amount of washing
and scrubbing was about to remove it. Prisoners hadn't been housed in these
cells since 1966, after a Supreme Court moratorium on the death penalty had so
overloaded the place that its inhabitants had been moved to the larger Ellis Unit.
A later ruling by the court — which determined the whole business to be cruel
and unusual and thus unconstitutional — had shut down the place for good.

Sometimes convicts on the squad balked at going in the cells because of the
century of condemned men that waited there; many believed that this old prison
was full of more of the dead than the living. But getting a crew to clean the cells
was a piece of cake compared to taking them into the adjoining room.

Ol' Brewer and another inmate looked at me and knew that I was about to
tell them to come with me.

"I done had to go in there the last time," the other inmate said. He pointed to
the others. "Somebody else ought to have to go, Boss. I done had to go last time."

I nodded. "And you did such a damn fine job," I told him, "I wanted you
special for this time."

The others laughed at that, and Ol' Brewer grinned. Which wasn't uncommon;
he grinned almost all of the time. He was the best-natured convict I ever saw.
Everybody — officers and inmates — called him Ol' Brewer; he was probably in
his early thirties, so he wasn't old. What he was, was big: around six feet six inches
tall, carrying too much weight on his huge frame. He had bad feet — probably
because of his excessive poundage — and limped along, towering over other
convicts. I'd sometimes see him in the upper yard when it was full of inmates,
lumbering through and above the flock of white uniforms, a creature marooned
in a society too diminutive and graceful for what he had to offer.

Ol' Brewer was as black as God could make a man, and the contrast between
his prison whites and that deep, glossy ebony was almost too dazzling to take in
all at once. His teeth were as white as the uniform, and when he grinned, which
he did most of the time, it seemed to bring it all into better focus.

He had been on the upper-yard squad for all the three years that I had been
at the Walls, and was known to everybody when I hired on. I asked him once how
long he had been in, and he had answered with his customary brevity: "Long
time, Boss." His voice was deep and mellow, like a slow-moving river. I'm sure
that if I had then asked him how much longer he had to be there, he would have

said the same thing. Long time. Which, in prison lingo, could mean anywhere from one year to sixty.

I took a deep breath before I opened the door to the next room. I didn't like going in there any more than the convicts did. The first time I crossed that threshold, I had known what would be there, bolted to the floor. But the knowledge hadn't diminished the reality of it. The light had inched across it as the door opened wider, and it was sitting there much closer and larger than I had expected, like a massive bed that takes up most of a bedroom. It reminded me then — and it always would thereafter — of a lion that had just finished devouring its prey, not caring in the least that someone was watching. Not threatened. Too dignified and powerful and unconcerned even to blink.

It was constructed of heavy oak, with thick leather straps to secure the condemned man's ankles, wrists and chest. It sat tall and perfectly upright in the

DOOR TO THE EXECUTION CHAMBER

exact center of the small room. A thick electric cable emerged from the window behind it, from the smaller room back there. The head harness, where the massive voltage was applied, hung limply over the top. A death row inmate had built it long ago — but only after his sentence had been commuted to life.

The three of us kept our distance.

"Jesus," the other inmate said when he looked at it. He always said that, every time I made him go in there. Ol' Brewer looked at it, too. He wasn't grinning now.

Every convict in the Walls — and probably every convict in the entire Texas prison system — knew the stories about the chair. The tales ran the gamut from hearsay to fact. Everyone knew the story about the lights all over Huntsville going dim during executions. There were tales about infamous condemned men, like Humpy Ross, a hunchbacked cuss who required two applications of voltage before he would die. The inmates told, too, about the stench that lingered in the room after every execution, a putrid odor of burned flesh. That last story was, by all accounts, true.

They enjoyed spinning yarns about the chair and the former inhabitants of the cells a few feet away from it. But at the heart of each story was a sense of sorrow and sympathy, and of course, the eternal question of justice. Never mind whether the condemned man had had an adequate lawyer. Many of the convicts believed that executions were never right.

They must have sensed a brotherhood with whatever ghosts might languish here. It was certainly a place where ghosts might abide. Dank and dark and cold and empty, in the most remote corner of the Walls. Locked up. Forgotten.

——

NOT TOO MANY WEEKS BEFORE, LIEUTENANT CAUTHEN HAD CALLED ME OFF THE yard and said that a sergeant was bringing a bunch of officer trainees from the dining hall. I was to take them out to the death house and show them around. He took a long pull from his Tab, and another from his cigarette, and told me the sergeant would stay in the yard till we got back.

I led the trainees past the searcher's desk and the gleaming brass bars of the bull ring, and down the long cellblock of the old East Building. Inside the death house, the trainees looked into the eight cells, but it didn't take long for the cocky one — there was always a cocky one — to cut to the chase.

"Where's Old Sparky?" he asked.

I opened the door.

They were all younger even than I was — some barely out of high school — and had of course never seen anything like this. They stood quietly, looking at the electric chair with the same dumbfounded expression that everybody wears when they first see it.

"Anybody want to touch it?" I asked

Nobody said yes. Three of the boys took a step back. Finally the cocky one thrust out his scrawny chest. "Hell," he said, "I ain't afraid to touch it." And he did, lightly and quickly, tapping the tip of one finger against the oak armrest.

He wore the self-satisfied look of someone who has done something of importance, then set his crew-cut head to bobbing like a fishing cork on a windy day.

The others nodded too. A couple of them slapped his back.

"Why don't you have a seat?" I said.

The room grew awfully quiet. His grin changed a little, and he looked harder at the chair.

"It won't bite," I told him.

"I guess I know that," he said, and looked back at his confederates. He thought a moment, then made his decision.

"Hell, yeah!" he said. He stepped forward.

"Do I just ... sit down?"

I nodded: "Just sit right down."

He turned and lowered himself gingerly onto the corner of the seat. It took him a few seconds to work up the courage to scoot further back, then he pressed his palms on the armrests. A few of the guys applauded. He smiled and winked.

"Ain't nothing to it," he said, his voice almost as sure and robust as it had been before he sat down.

There was an old exhaust fan just above the chair. I had turned that fan on before, when I had taken a clean-up crew out there, and knew that, because it was so seldom used and needed lubricating, it would make a god-awful racket.

I was standing next to the switch.

When that fan clattered on, the cocky kid lurched out of the chair and landed a good three feet away. The following Tuesday, I felt fortunate that my squad had only dust to clean up.

———

I WATCHED OL' BREWER AND THE OTHER INMATE AS THEY SWEPT THE RUBBER MATS on the floor of the death chamber and then scrub down the door frames. When they were finished, they both looked at the chair again, each hoping I wouldn't say his name. Since the other inmate had complained about having to come in here twice in a row, I decided to give Brewer the honor this week.

"Go on and dust it off," I told him.

He knew I wouldn't let him get by with a half-hearted effort, so he cautiously rubbed down the wood, then the straps and the head harness and, finally, the electrodes.

He stepped back and grinned, obviously happy that it was over.

The other convicts had gathered in the doorway. I tried to use my most authoritative voice.

"Have a seat in the chair, Brewer."

He looked at me, his eyes wide, not a trace of his trademark smile evident. He had almost certainly never disobeyed an officer during his entire incarceration, and he obviously wasn't sure whether I was joking or serious.

"No, thank you, Boss Willett," he finally said, his slow, deep voice full of courtesy and dignity. "I think I'd rather not."

Everybody roared with laughter, and none louder than me.

I remembered that young officer in training, and reached a conclusion that has many times been proven to be true: Old inmates are generally quicker on the uptake than new boots.

007

"JUST SITTING HERE WAITING FOR THAT OLD TEN o'clock to come, huh, Mr. Willett?"

Inmate Roach sat down beside me on the low brick wall outside the major's office. He tilted two cigarettes out of his pack, but I got one from my own pocket. He lit it for me, and from his own blew a long, slow line of smoke into the humid evening.

"Fixing to go home," he said, drawing it out, getting the most out of it. "Get out of that uniform, put on some good duds, and head out for a party." He leaned forward and winked. "I can see it in your eyes. Hell, I don't blame you. If I could, I'd go with you."

He looked around, at the wide upper yard that was almost empty now. At the searcher's desk off to our left. At the last few convicts walking toward the showers in the west yard. Most of them had worked in the kitchen or the textile mill, and had just gotten off.

"But hell" — he squinted, as if actually making a decision — "I think I'll just stay in tonight."

He was maybe a couple of years older than me, and was in good shape. He talked about playing a lot of baseball when he was a kid. We often discussed the Astros, and he was a member of the Walls inmate team, the Tigers. Because he was so young, we were smoking decent cigarettes, not the unfiltered Camels that old convicts smoked, or the ones they rolled themselves using the coarse state-issued tobacco that stained their fingers yellow. Roach hadn't yet had time to get old in here. I hoped he wouldn't.

Steve Roach was Major Murdock's bookkeeper, and he was a damned good one. I worked for Captain Lindsey, and since the captain and the major shared an office, I saw Roach a lot. Bookkeepers were convicts who had good number sense and good heads on their shoulders. Each building had one, and they all worked for the major. The building bookkeepers took care of the paperwork, tasks like typing reports for officers. They maintained the count boards, answered the phone, and relayed messages to the officers. They did an important job for Major Murdock, and the bookkeeper who worked in his office was the top of the crop. That was Steve Roach.

He set his plastic soap container on the bricks beside him, leaned back, and looked up at the last light of a still, cloudless summer afternoon.

"Man," he said, "I sure wish I could get back out on them streets, and have me a good time." He grinned. He might have been looking at the sky, but what he was seeing was over a hundred miles away. In Dallas.

"I used to know how to party."

I looked at my watch. Second shift would be over soon.

"Yeah," I said, "there's an art to it, all right."

He laughed, and we fell into one of those silences that are not uncommon on pleasant nights when there's just a hint of a breeze. A few gnats buzzed around, and the flowers in the bed behind us were in bloom. Warden Husbands loved flowers, so they were planted everywhere they could be.

Roach and I smoked our cigarettes and stayed quiet. After a while, the convicts came back from their showers.

"Goodnight, Boss," one told me as he passed.

We watched them go off toward their cells in the East and West buildings, and soon we had the big yard to ourselves. I finished my smoke and snubbed the butt in the flowerbed.

"What are you down here for?" I asked Roach. It wasn't a question that I often asked convicts, but tonight seemed the right time. He had told me several times about growing up around Dallas. He had talked about his family, and had even introduced me to his mom and dad one day when I was working visitation. And, of course, he was close to my age and liked baseball. Like me — if I'd hung out with the wrong crowd in high school.

He leaned forward and rolled the stub of his cigarette between his fingers. He blew on it. Made the end glow bright.

"Some shit up home," he said. "In one of the bad parts of Dallas. Some of us were just riding down the street, and we got into an argument with some guys in another car. We all pulled into a side street. A guy got shot." He flicked the butt into the bed. "Killed."

His eyes got wider then. He looked at me.

"I didn't do it," he said. "I was just there when I should've been somewhere else."

This wasn't a new refrain. Damned near every convict in the place would profess his innocence. Some actually believed the words as they said them. Hell, maybe some of them were innocent. Sheer numbers indicated that some of them would be.

Then Roach added something I had never heard from any other convict. "But I sure as hell done enough other things bad enough to get sent down here. So I can't bitch too much." He stretched again, and dug out another cigarette.

We talked a little baseball, and the next shift came on.

"Well, Mr. Willett," he said as he stood up, "have yourself a real good time tonight and drink one for me." He headed toward the showers.

I did party that night, and I thought about Roach from time to time. Under different circumstances, we could have taken in an Astros game together and gotten a beer.

There are walls between people everywhere, I guess. But in the place where I worked, they were real walls.

A COUPLE OF WEEKS LATER I WAS WORKING UTILITY IN THE FIVE BUILDING WHEN I heard a commotion. I looked in one of the tanks and saw two convicts. One picked up a broom and cold-cocked the other.

"Break it up!" I yelled, and they did. The one who had been at the receiving end didn't need much encouragement. Captain Lindsey had me lock up the one who'd delivered the blow.

I wrote the necessary report, an IOC. Roach typed it, and I signed it. As the third shift was relieving me, he came out of the office.

"I misspelled a word on that IOC, Mr. Willett," he said. "You know how the major is about misspelled words."

I did.

"I know you're in a hurry to get out of here. If you'll sign this blank IOC, I'll retype it and put it on the major's desk."

I looked at my watch and thought about my date that night. I signed the paper, thanked him, and went home.

The next afternoon I went to roll call, then headed to the yard as utility officer. A couple of the major's bookkeepers from the Count Room next to his office were sitting on the edge of the flowerbed.

"I believe the major mentioned that he wanted to see you when you got here, Mr. Willett," one of them said. He smiled. So did the other one.

I asked if the major was in his office.

The first inmate nodded. "I do believe he is. Let me just check." He got up, knocked on the major's screen door, and stuck his head in.

"Tell him to get his ass in here," came the major's voice. Loud. Convicts in front of the chapel turned to see what was happening.

I went in.

"You wanted to see me, Major?"

He leaned back in his office chair, so far back that I was afraid he might tip. He didn't. His eyes were narrowed to slits; his forehead was a grid of lines.

"Willett," he said, "would you mind explaining this?" He tossed a piece of paper in my direction.

I lifted it from his desk. It was an IOC.

It was dated the day before, was addressed to the major, and consisted of a single line, neatly typed.

Major Murdock is a punk, it said.

"Well?" he asked.

"Major," I managed to say. The rest came stumbling out. "I didn't write … I mean, type. No, write. This." I jabbed the paper with my finger.

"Is that your signature? That's all I want to know?"

I looked at it again, as if it could have magically changed since the last time I had looked at it.

"Yes, sir," I sighed. "It is."

His piercing blue eyes widened a bit. He leaned back again.

"Then you think I'm a punk. Is that right?"

"Major…" I started.

Captain Lindsey, who had come in without my seeing him, was the first to laugh, followed by the two bookkeepers. Then the major himself cracked a smile.

"I'll kill that damned Roach," I said.

"Well," the major said, "you could do that, I guess." He sat behind his desk like a judge. "But what you ought to do is never again in your lifetime — at the very least, in a prison — sign a blank sheet of paper."

I never again did.

Captain Lindsey and Major Murdock made me the payroll officer of the Walls not long after that, in charge of distributing the books of script that inmates used to buy things at the commissary. I still saw Steve Roach from time to time, and we continued to talk in the yard. Mostly about baseball.

008

MY SHIFT WAS ABOUT TO BEGIN WHEN THE FIRST SHOT was fired. My friend Wayne Scott and a sergeant, Bruce Noviskie, had decided to investigate a disturbance in the prison education department, at the top of a three-story building that had no name. Later, it would be named after people who died there.

As the two officers walked up the long ramp, toward the glass doors, the first bullet zipped through Wayne's shirt, the left side, about four inches above his belt. Another bullet lodged itself in the heel of Noviskie's shoe.

I arrived a few minutes after they'd scrambled to safety. The prison was in chaos. Supervisors who I had never seen lose their composure were shaken, unsure what to do. People were running. Blotches of sweat, unusual even for July, stained the uniforms of both inmates and officers. At the armpits. At the collars. On the backs.

I joined a group at the searcher's desk. Nobody knew who was firing the guns, or what hostages might be up there. But we knew this: The upper yard had to be cleared, and quickly. The shots had been fired from the double doors at the top of the three-story ramp, and from that vantage point the shooter had a clear view of everything in the yard. Anybody in the open area would be easy pickings, even for a lousy marksman.

Whoever had orchestrated this plan had chosen wisely. The third floor had no windows, and there was only one way in or out. The third floor was a fortress.

———

FATHER O'BRIEN, THE CATHOLIC CHAPLAIN, WALKED ACROSS THE EMPTY UPPER yard with the same confident stride that he would use to walk to lunch on a normal day. Out in the open, he looked neither to the right or the left, but straight ahead. Toward the ramp and the glass doors at its top.

He didn't stop when he got to the building, or even look up toward the doors, but started up the tall concrete ramp. When he reached the top, one of the glass doors opened slightly, and he slipped through like a drop of water absorbed by a sponge.

In not too many minutes, inmates started exiting the education department, a few at a time, running down the ramp like rats escaping a burning building. We waved them over to us by the searcher's desk. Whoever held the guns upstairs was thinning the herd, choosing the best hostages.

We shook down the released inmates, one at a time, to make sure they hadn't been sent out with weapons. Then we took them to the barber shop or one of the offices, where they'd be questioned about what they had seen or heard.

Someone said that the priest had volunteered to go. The convict I was shaking down trembled slightly. My hands had been on his shoulder, and they stayed there. The convict shook again, the kind of tremor that comes when you remember a bad thing.

"He went right up there," he said.

I nodded, and continued to frisk him.

"I sure wouldn't go back up there," the convict said. "If I had me a choice."

I finished my search, and pushed him along to another officer.

"You ain't no priest, neither," the next inmate said.

The first convict grinned — not the usual cocky prison smirk, but a nervous grin, full of terror and relief. "Naw," he said, as the other officer led him to the barbershop. "I ain't no priest."

The next prisoner stood in front of me, facing away with his arms outstretched. As I frisked him, he spoke just loud enough that I could hear.

"What's gonna happen, Boss?"

A cloudless summer sky stretched out over the Walls. The empty yard spread out beside us. The big hospital rose up on one side, the long Four and Five Building beside it. The three-story building's glass doors were closed. Inside, a desk or table was shoved up against them.

"Damned if I know," I said.

A SEMBLANCE OF ORDER FELL INTO PLACE. WARDEN HUSBANDS ORDERED US TO lock up all the inmates that we did still control. So we brought them in from work, or from the chow hall, or from wherever they happened to be, and put them in their cells. Those housed in the East and West Buildings were brought around behind the three-story building via the west yard, and those in Four and Five were herded quickly, close to the building's walls.

Before long, scraps of information began trickling down. We learned that a telephone line was open between the education department and Warden Husband's office. Somebody said that all the system's top administrators were either already in the warden's office or were on their way there. Somebody else had said that W. J Estelle, the director, was in San Antonio, but was on his way back to Huntsville.

Then the names of the armed inmates started flying around in the hot afternoon like electricity. Carrasco and Cuevas and Dominiquez. For a while the triumvirate was referred to as a single entity, the three names breathed out like one sound. But then it became apparent that the planning, the brains, and the total authority resided in just one of them. Then the entire predicament was embodied in a single word.

Carrasco.

I knew him as a porter in the chapel. He walked with a cane and worked for Father O'Brien. He was of average height, perhaps a little taller than most Mexican men, and was slightly overweight. He never smiled. We learned his criminal history through the grapevine. He had been a powerful figure in the Mexican equivalent of the Mafia, and had been captured and incarcerated in Mexico. There had been a daring helicopter escape from a prison in Guadalajara, then

he had been apprehended again after a shoot-out in a Texas motel. He had pleaded guilty to attempted murder, reportedly in exchange for the release of his wife, Rosa, and ended up at the Walls with a life sentence. And with a pronounced limp and a cane, results of the shoot-out.

I knew Ignacio Curevas from my stints of chow-line duty; he was a waiter in the inmate dining hall. I had never heard of Rudy Dominguez.

Of course, the three had hostages. Possibly some inmates were being held, but there was no doubt that civilians were, too. Free-world hostages would provide considerably more leverage than convicts. The teachers in the education department. The librarians. Bobby Heard, a fellow officer and a good guy, had been on duty in there, and he hadn't shown up anywhere else. So he was there.

Bobby was wearing the gray prison-guard uniform that convicts hate. I figured he was in the most precarious situation of all.

———

FATHER O'BRIEN CAME BACK DOWN AND WALKED RIGHT PAST US TO WARDEN Husband's office. He was holding a piece of paper.

"Demands," somebody called. "He's got their demands."

The word fluttered like a bird. Through the bull ring. At the searcher's desk.

"They ain't going to give in to any demands," somebody said. The whole assemblage nodded at that, with the uniformity of a Greek chorus. Even some of the inmates being frisked nodded.

"When Mr. Estelle gets here," somebody said, "he'll tell 'em where they can stuff their goddamned demands." Then, for the first time, there was a little laughter.

A bed count was made, and it was determined exactly who the inmate captives were. Four convicts were officially listed as hostages, but we all wondered if this was indeed the case. We wondered if they were being held against their will, or if they had agreed to stay.

Later, Mr. Estelle arrived from San Antonio. There was a great commotion at the entrance when he got there. Several men tried to tell him things at the same time. Somebody said the media was already camped outside.

PREVIOUS PAGES: THE RAMP TO THE EDUCATION DEPARTMENT

Sergeant Black, a big-bellied jovial fellow, leaned against one of the long tables in the bull ring. His wife managed the Parkwood apartments, where I shared a unit with Ronnie Rozelle. I asked the sergeant what he figured would happen.

"How the hell should I know?" he said. He looked down the hall at the hullabaloo attending Mr. Estelle's arrival, then at all the men assembled in this room. "I ain't never been in nothing like this," he said. And he had been here forever.

"How do you think they got guns in here?" I asked.

He thought about it, then shook his head. "Ain't no telling," he finally said. He looked around the room, at the throng of gray uniforms. Then back at me. "But somebody's ass will damn sure end up in a sling about that."

We spent much of the rest of the afternoon looking up at the third floor, at the double glass doors with furniture pressed next to them.

"I guess there's some ladies up there," I said.

"I'd bet on it," said Sergeant Black. Until recently, very few women had worked in the Walls except in the front offices. The women up there now would be teachers and librarians, people ill-equipped to face what was possibly happening to them. In fragments of conversation, I heard the word "rape."

We were all standing this quiet, uneventful vigil when Father O'Brien and an inmate carrying a television set and several pairs of handcuffs, walked through us and out into the yard. We gathered closer and watched them go up the ramp.

"What the hell?" somebody said.

One of the doors opened just wide enough that the television could be pulled in.

"What the hell's going on?" Somebody else this time.

Before the inmates even made it back to the bull ring, we'd heard the rumor that the captors had demanded many things, including more guns, bulletproof vests, and walkie-talkies.

Everybody grumbled about that. And about the television set. And even about how these guys had gotten guns — or at least *a* gun — into the Walls in the first place. Then the grumbling died down as each man ran a mental inventory of times he might have been sleepy, or not especially vigilant.

"This ain't worth a shit," somebody said.

The statement was met with nods and damn rights. Mr. Estelle was calling the plays now, and nobody liked this first one. Surely, I thought, he wouldn't give in to these men. But the television and the handcuffs had gone up there as quickly as room service in a hotel.

"Bobby's up there," somebody said.

And that explained everything. We all looked up at the third floor and didn't say anything more about how things ought to be done.

WHEN SUPPER WAS SERVED, AS USUAL, IN THE INMATE DINING HALL DIRECTLY under the education department, no alternate route was available except to march the convicts into the building in full view of whoever was up there behind the glass doors. The men traversed the area as quickly as they were allowed and sat down to what turned out to be the last hot meal they would eat for a long while. Carrasco, we would later learn, became agitated by the noise in the dining hall below him, and told the warden over the phone that he believed an assault was being organized down there. Warden Husbands assured him that the racket was only the normal sounds of dishwashers and hundreds of men. But Carraso wanted quiet, and he was in a position to get what he wanted. From then on, throughout the siege, the inmates' meals would come in paper bags, "johnny sacks" handed to them in their cells.

Finally, that night, everyone was showered, and fed, and locked up.

I wondered when the siege would end. As darkness fell on Huntsville and the Walls, there was nothing to do but sit and wait. This was about the time that I had intended to begin celebrating my graduation from college. Instead I sat with all the other officers whose lives had been put on hold.

Somebody called my name. Captain Lindsey motioned to me.

"Glenn Johnson just had a heart attack up there," he said. He didn't even nod toward the three-story building. By then, "up there" meant only one thing. "They just called the warden and told him to send up some convicts to get him. You get on over to the hospital, in case they need to send him to Huntsville Memorial. You ride in the ambulance with him." He pointed his finger at me. "You stay right beside him, all the time. Don't let anybody get to him except medical people and his family. Understand?"

"Yes, sir," I told him, already plotting my course so I wouldn't have to cross the yard. Mr. Johnson was the education and recreation consultant at the Walls. I liked him.

The inmates took him across the yard to the unit hospital, where he was kept only long enough to determine that he could be moved. He was awake, but in obvious pain.

Huntsville Memorial Hospital was only a few blocks away, on the other side of the courthouse square. During the short ride, I wanted badly to ask Mr. Johnson what was going on up on the third floor. He must have read the question in my eyes. He leaned up a little to speak.

"It's a bad situation," he said. And that was all.

At the hospital, a doctor examined him, determined that whatever had happened hadn't been a heart attack, and told a nurse to admit him. Not long after he was moved to a room, a prison official went in to talk to him. To ask questions, I supposed, about the third floor. Where everybody was. How they were being treated. How the hostages were holding up.

I stood in the hall and waited for the official to come out, in case he had orders for me.

He didn't. He just walked to the elevator and was gone. I leaned against the wall beside the door to Mr. Johnson's room and continued doing what Captain Lindsey told me to do.

A nurse brought me a chair. "You can't stand up all night," she told me. She was about my mother's age.

I thanked her, and sat in the chair. A little later, I leaned it back against the wall.

Sometime before daylight, the nurse went off duty and stopped to see me on her way out. She was holding her purse and a plastic bag, which probably held empty containers from her supper.

"You doing all right?" she asked. Her East Texas drawl was rich; she hadn't wandered too far away from her birthplace.

"Yes, ma'am," I told her.

She smiled. Then she pursed her lower lip a little. Nobody in Huntsville would have been able to sustain a smile for very long just then.

"I hope y'all get all this taken care of real soon," she said. "And nobody gets hurt."

She added the next thing quickly.

"The guards and hostages, I mean."

She said goodnight, and I sat alone in the hallway, waiting in my hard chair for somebody to relieve me. Waiting for morning.

I knew Bobby Heard was waiting for it, too.

009

EARLY THE NEXT MORNING, WHEN I GOT BACK TO THE
Walls, I learned that the identities of the employee
hostages had been released to the press. They were
seven women and three men. Except for Bobby Heard,
they were teachers, librarians, and employees of the
school district.

One at a time, bound hand and foot, the captives
would sit in a chair on top of other furniture just
inside the glass doors. The hostage's back was to us, so
we sometimes didn't know who it was. But we could
usually tell when it was Bobby Heard. He was in the
chair a lot.

Outside the walls, a media army had set up camp,
their vehicles cluttering the narrow streets, antennas
sprouting into the hot East Texas sky like weeds.
Behind the media were the onlookers — hundreds at
any given time — sitting in cars or in the backs of
pickups, or just standing and watching. Waiting.

Sometime that morning — we weren't watching
clocks or wristwatches any more; all of our attention
was on the double doors — Father O'Brien crossed
the yard a second time and walked up the ramp
into the makeshift fortress. Carrasco had told Warden
Husbands to send him the day before, to get the
demands, but this time the idea had been Father
O'Brien's; he wanted to comfort anybody who might
need him. We assumed that he would come back

down a little later, but he didn't. So we added one more hostage to the list.

Shifts of duty dissolved. As the siege wore on, we were all at the Walls all the time. We rested when we could, slept wherever we could stretch out, and spent countless hours doing nothing. Waiting.

After Carrasco groused about the noise from the inmate dining hall, Warden Husbands decided not to use it. The prospect of ferrying johnny sacks to every tank in every building set us to grumbling; we saw it as one more concession to the gunmen. What we didn't know was that Carrasco had threatened to kill a hostage if the racket didn't stop. That hostage would have been Bobby Heard.

So we delivered johnnys, and the prisoners in their cells found the room service considerably more amusing than we did. But it didn't take long for them to get over the irony of the situation, and to tire of the mundane offerings in the paper sacks. Our prisoners were used to hot meals of a quality that surprises many outsiders — fresh meat and produce that was, more likely than not, raised and grown on prison farms. By comparison, the johnny sacks seemed like bread and water.

Food, though, was only the beginning of the inmates' complaints. After the dining hall was shut down, prisoners were kept in their tanks, or in their individual cells, all the time. No transient inmates were brought into the unit for the duration of the siege. All parole and release operations were moved to the Diagnostic Unit.

Boredom set in, and tension in the cells grew thick. One day a guard assigned to East Building watched a paper airplane float down from the upper tier. It sailed lazily through the still, hot air and came to rest on the concrete floor of the main run. He picked it up, unfolded it, and found this note scribbled on the paper:

> *I am holding my cell partner hostage. If I don't get some hot food soon I will kill him.*

We felt the frustration too.

The days dragged on, and it became apparent that the siege could continue forever. We returned to shift work. Though the shifts were twelve hours instead of the usual eight, each was a carbon copy of the one before and the one that would follow. When we weren't doing specific chores — carrying food to the tanks, relieving an officer so he could eat, or getting counts, a simple task under these conditions — we would plop in the shade to rest, and our uniforms, every fiber of every thread soaked, would dry, leaving white, crusty blotches. Then there would be another job, and more sweat. The cycle repeated itself several times a day, like an oven continually turned on and off.

Irritability crept in. We got mad. At Carrasco and his cohorts, of course. And at the inmates who sat in their cells, waiting for food to be handed in to them. And at each other, if only because we were close by. And at Mr. Estelle, for letting this situation fester. Of course, none of us knew how to free the hostages, either.

One morning early in the second week, Captain Lindsey approached me. "Willett," he said, "the warden has decided that the inmates are gonna get their script books."

Two things flew immediately through my mind: first, the absolute stupidity of such a procedure under such abnormal circumstances; and second, the realization that as payroll officer, I would have to carry out that procedure. And not by counting out script books over a desk as I did every week, but by taking them to individual cells.

I asked what I considered a good question.

"What are they supposed to do with them, once they get them?"

Script was only good in the commissary, and it was closed. Even if it were open, the convicts couldn't get to it. They were locked up.

The captain let the hint of a smile work its way into the corner of his mouth. "Warden Husbands has also decided that we'll open the commissary back up," he said. "Officers will collect the convicts' script, buy their stuff for them, and deliver it to their cells, just like the row tenders usually do."

I bit my lip, nodded, and might have even said "Yes, sir." Then I watched the immediate future flicker in my brain like a movie. I'd walk all over the unit, handing out script. When that was done, I'd deliver candy bars, animal crackers, Cokes, and fans.

It didn't take many visits to many cells to convince me that the routine would wear me out. At each cell, I had to squat down and slide the computer printout under the door, hand the inmate a pen so he could sign his name, get my pen back, and slide an ink pad under the door so he could press his thumbprint beside his signature. He slid the pad back to me, and I handed him his book of script. Then his cellmate stepped up, and I did it all again. By the time I got to the end of the first row, my back and legs ached from the squatting.

I felt like I'd been the catcher in a doubleheader.

As I moved to the next row, I did a little arithmetic. There were forty-six rows in the unit, not including solitary, which I wouldn't pay until they were returned to the general population. Each row consisted of at least twenty cells, with two men in each one. Not every inmate drew on his account every week — some didn't even have money in their accounts — but the majority did. Add to that the sixty-six inmates in the outside trusty quarters, and I was looking at a hell of a job.

Hours later, I finally finished the eleven rows in East Building, and moved to West — but not before finding Captain Lindsey and telling him I needed help. He looked at his watch and commenced calculations of his own. At this rate, it would take the better part of a week to get everybody paid. So he located an unfortunate officer and told him to give me a hand.

Two days later, backs and legs aching, we were finished, and for once I felt I'd earned my pay. Before the siege, I often compared my job in the Walls to my old job at the gas station, and sometimes caught myself grinning at how easy I had it here in the prison. But that late afternoon, after hours of squatting and standing up, over and over, I felt like I had changed every tire on every vehicle in Huntsville.

The waiting, though, was worse than the aches. Carrasco began losing hostages. On Sunday, just before dawn, an inmate, Henry Escamilla, dove beside the captive sitting in the chair, through the plate glass door at the top of the ramp and rolled down into the yard. By the time he got to the bull ring, he was a bloody mess and was taken to the unit hospital. Later, Carrasco called the warden's office and said that Mrs. House, a librarian, had suffered a heart attack and would be released. She was carried down on a stretcher, as Mr. Johnson had been, and was transported to the Huntsville hospital. Then, on the second Friday afternoon, a librarian, Mrs. Woodman, was sent down. We figured she was relaying demands. We thought everything would come to a head soon.

But the gunmen stayed up there, still with nine hostages. And we stayed frustrated.

Our dispositions didn't improve when we watched Carrasco's demands being met. He wanted free-world clothes for his two compadres and himself, and not cheap stuff — Nunn Bush shoes; only Nunn Bush would do. So he got them. We watched convicts haul carry-out orders from Huntsville restaurants up there; no johnny sacks for these guys. And we all watched quietly as the helmets that Carrasco had ordered were carried up. They'd been fabricated according to his exact specifications in the metal shop: Huge bulky dark things, with thick steel curled up at the bottoms to rest on the wearer's shoulders. They looked like something out of a low-budget movie set in the Middle Ages, and we had significant doubts regarding their practicality. But those doubts didn't lessen our resentment that those sons of bitches were getting what they wanted, when they wanted it.

THE NIGHT BEFORE THE LAST DAY, A THUNDERSTORM RUMBLED THROUGH Huntsville. A bolt of lightning blew out a main transformer at midnight, casting the entire unit into darkness. Carrasco, of course, suspected the worst: that the power had been cut off in preparation for an assault, but somebody — either Mr. Estelle or the warden — managed to mollify him.

By the time I got to work, the lights were back on. Carrasco, his two confederates, and their hostages — what was left of them — were still encamped on the third floor. I spent most of my shift trying to catch up on paperwork in my small payroll office in Five Building. Then word came down from Major Murdock that each inmate was to be locked in his individual cell, not simply contained in the tanks.

For once the convicts didn't balk or grumble when we racked them up. They knew that something was about to happen. Any sense of inmate loyalty to the gunmen on the third floor had faded with each day of the standoff. By now the convicts just wanted the siege to be over. To them, the prospect of a resolution smelled like fresh air and hot food.

Later that afternoon, Mr. Chance, the security officer in charge of Five Building, answered the phone. When he finished talking, he walked downstairs and locked the only door to the building. Mr. Chance was older than the rest of us, a big man over six feet tall, with a stern voice and a slow, intentional way of doing things. He had taught most of us how to be good guards, and when he told us something, we listened. What he told us, now, was to stay put.

"No one is allowed on the yard," he said. "As of right now." Whatever Mr. Estelle had on tap would happen there.

I desperately wanted to see what was going on. Then I remembered a pipe chase, an open area that housed pipes and electrical conduits. It was on the side of the building next to the yard, and I thought its large vent housings might offer the view I craved. I made my way down a narrow hallway that led to the housing. And there it was: a ringside seat.

I scrunched down and got my bearings. I could see the entire upper yard as evening fell on the unit, sending a dark shadow along the red brick walls, across the front of the white hospital. Over the bull ring, the big clock was barely visible in the shadows. The only new addition to the tableau was parked at the base of the ramp: an armored car.

I stared at it for a long moment. My heart sank as I imagined the gunmen driving out of the sallyport and into freedom, their hostages still captive. For now, it was eerily quiet.

I didn't have long to ponder anything more.

"Mr. Willett," Mr. Chance's voice rumbled down the dark hall behind me. "Is that you?"

"Yes sir," I answered softly, so as not to be heard in the yard.

"Get yourself out of there," he said. "Major Murdock just called me and said he could see an officer clear as day in a vent housing."

THERE WAS NOTHING TO DO NOW BUT SIT AND WAIT. IT GREW DARKER OUTSIDE, and I wondered, along with everyone else in Five Building, what was going on out there.

Then we heard a series of muffled popping sounds, like firecrackers going off in the distance. There was a silence, then another flurry of pops. More silence, then louder shots. Mr. Chance and I looked at each other.

"Pistols," we said at the same time.

Then there was a longer silence than I could stand.

"I'll go back up to that housing to see what happened," I said.

"No, you won't."

"Then let me go outside." I cocked my head to listen.

"It's over now."

VENT HOUSINGS FOR THE PIPE CHASE

"You ain't going nowhere," he said.

He listened long enough to confirm that no more shots were coming. He sighed and unlocked the front door.

I hurried around the corner of the captain's office and into the yard. The armored car was still parked in the same place, but the upper yard was no longer empty. People were everywhere. Two officers pushed past me carrying Father O'Brien on a stretcher.

I worked my way through the sea of officers. Everyone was yelling. Everyone was running. It was as if the wide, open place that had been still and empty for so long was overcompensating for it now. Another stretcher, bearing one of the women, was rushed toward the hospital.

One inmate lay near the edge of the ramp. Water mixed with blood was everywhere. On the ramp and on the ground.

Two more inmates lay in a heap on the ramp. The first one I came to was Carrasco, his body stretched in a pool of the bloody water on the incline, his head split open. Dominiquez was dead, too, on the first landing of the ramp.

"This one's still alive!" somebody shouted. The words rang through the night like a siren. Everyone converged on Cuevas, the waiter in the inmate chow hall. By all appearances, he hadn't been injured, and I suspect he survived only because so many people were on the scene. More than a few of the officers would have gladly added his name to the roster of the dead.

A huge apparatus stood at the bottom of the ramp. It had been constructed of chalkboards and lined with the thickest law books in the library. The thing was held together with masking tape and ropes, and what was left of it was bullet-ridden and splashed with blood. Whatever had happened, had happened inside it.

Officers stripped the clothing away from Carrasco and Dominiquez, to check for weapons and, doubtless, to get them out of the expensive suits that we had resented for almost two weeks. A couple of the officers were using knives to cut the clothing away, and someone lifted Carrasco's body up to pull the garments free. When he dropped him back to the ramp, his head hit the concrete with a sickening thud.

I helped wherever it looked like I was needed, and did whatever I was told to do. The chaos in the yard whirled around me; guards and policemen and men in civilian clothes — FBI agents and Texas Rangers probably — brushed past. At one point, I saw Mr. Estelle, who looked as downhearted as I had ever seen a man look. He glared, stone-faced, directly in front of him.

"Willett," Captain Lindsey called. "Get over to the searcher's desk and wait for me."

When he got there, he pointed to a pile of bloody material that I knew used to be Carrasco's and Dominiquez's clothing.

"Go through it," he told us. "Every piece. Slow and careful."

I swallowed hard at the prospect. I had already seen more mutilation than I had counted on when I had begged Mr. Chance to let me go out into the yard.

I leaned down and picked up a soggy, bullet-ridden suit coat. The other men lifted other things. We probed every pocket and all along the stitching to make sure nothing was hidden. I had to wring some of the things out before I could inspect them.

"All of this isn't blood," I said. "Where'd all the water come from?"

"They sprayed 'em with a high-pressure hose," said one of the other guards. "To knock the thing over."

I kept at the task, wishing I was wearing gloves and a mask, and flicked away tiny particles of skin and bone when I came to them. When we were finished, Captain Lindsey told us to leave the clothes beside the searchers' desk. We laid them in a pile beside the gunmen's pistols and their three gothic helmets.

In a few minutes, Mr. Bobby Maggard, the assistant director, told Captain Lindsey he was taking the gunmen's items across the street to be locked in the vault of the prison administration building. The captain pointed at me, then at the things on the ground, then in the direction of the unit's front door.

Captain Lindsey, Dean Hamm and I followed Mr. Maggard, carrying the things past the brass bars of the bull ring, down the hallway past the warden's office, and out toward the Walls' front porch.

We opened the door. People filled the sidewalks, the street, and the lawn. The congregation extended up the hill, along the front wall and the warden's house, and down it, toward the courthouse square. Many of the people were reporters and photographers, but there were townspeople too, standing wide-eyed and frightened

CARRASCO HELMETS, GUNS, AND AMMUNITION

THE MAKESHIFT "TROJAN HORSE" USED AS A SHIELD IN THE ESCAPE ATTEMPT

of the official announcement they were waiting for. Everything that we had seen in the upper yard, they were only guessing.

When we stepped out on the porch, and the sprawling crowd caught their first glimpse of those helmets, they grew as quiet as if watching a flag being raised.

They stayed that way as we made our procession. As we walked down the steps, the crowd parted for us and we waded through. Mr. Maggard was in front; we stayed close behind. I kept my eyes facing forward. Nobody tried to touch the helmet I was carrying, but everybody watched as it went by.

We stowed the helmets and clothes and returned to the unit. The makeshift shield used by the gunmen — the newspapers would call it the Piñata, or the Trojan Horse — was dismantled and removed. The education department on the third floor looked like a demolition crew had worked on it. Books, tables, and chairs were everywhere. It was impossible to determine how much of the damage had been done during the siege because officers were already tearing the place apart, looking for weapons and explosives.

I watched as they went about their work, turning over tables and chairs, sliding whole rows of books off the library shelves. The books fell in heaps on the floor. I wondered if the place could ever be orderly again.

I wondered if, after this, anything or any of us could ever be the same.

MR. ESTELLE STOOD IN FRONT OF THE UNIT THAT NIGHT, FACING THE MICROPHONES, the flashbulbs, the television cameras, the reporters, the onlookers, the friends and family of hostages and guards — facing the world.

His voice broke when he announced that two of the hostages were dead: Mrs. Yvonne Beseda, a teacher, and Mrs. Julia Standley, a librarian. We learned later that Carrasco had handcuffed himself to Ms. Beseda, Dominguez to Ms. Standley, and Cuevas to Ms. Pollard. The gunmen had handcuffed Father O'Brien to the apparatus, and they forced their hostages down the ramp inside the makeshift shield.

Outside, a team of law-enforcement officers turned a high-pressure hose on the shield. When the hose burst, a shootout began.

Carrasco shot Ms. Beseda, then himself.

Dominguez shot Ms. Standley. A Texas Ranger shot him.

Father O'Brien was critically wounded. The remaining hostages were unharmed. Carrasco and Dominquez were dead, and the third gunman, Cuevas, was in custody.

Mr. Estelle told the crowd that he had never, at any time during the long ordeal, given any thought to letting the gunmen go free. For one thing, he told the somber, attentive crowd, he couldn't in good conscience release that brand of violence on the outside community. And for another, he owed his staff the assurance that any prisoner who took a hostage would not be provided a means of escape.

I appreciated that assurance. And for all the griping done among the ranks — and I did my share — I'm certain that Mr. Estelle's actions during those long, hot eleven days and nights were the correct ones, even though innocent lives were lost.

DIRECTOR W. J. ESTELLE ADDRESSING REPORTERS DURING THE SIEGE

We learned that Carrasco had been a hell of a planner. The three pistols that were the keystone of his scheme had been easily secured by accomplices in the free world, but had to be delivered to Carrasco inside the prison. That was the role of one Lawrence Hall, an outside trusty who worked as a houseboy in an assistant director's residence, across the street from the Walls. The guns were delivered to him when he was at the house alone. Hall took a ham out of the freezer. He hollowed it out, placed the .38 pistol inside it, wrapped it back up, and let the meat rot. One day, he returned to the unit and told the guard at the East Gate that he was delivering spoiled meat that the Missus wanted returned to the kitchen. One whiff on a hot, still afternoon provided sufficient proof, and Hall walked in with the weapon.

Later, Hall placed two .357's together and wrapped them in butcher paper, so that the package looked like meat. He put the package in a cardboard box, placed more spoiled meat on top, and once again carried his contraband through the East Gate. The bullets were delivered inside large cans that appeared to hold peaches.

Soon, the guns and ammunition were in the hands of Carrasco, the quiet porter in the chapel who hobbled with a cane. Once barricaded in the third floor, he cast the cane aside and moved around with no limp whatsoever. And there, he found the loud, confident voice that held the world's attention for almost two weeks.

After Mr. Estelle's announcement, the media and the rest of the crowd lingered awhile, then began to disperse. Major Murdock met with those of us that were going off our shift and told us what to expect the next morning. Before the prisoners could be released from their cells, he told us, we'd have to go over the entire unit, every nook and cranny, to make absolutely sure no contraband, like ammunition, was hidden.

Major Murdock was as tired as the rest of us. His short frame seemed to sag in his gray, sweat-stained uniform. His words came out slower than usual. Carrasco had hated him more than anyone else, and on the phone with reporters the inmate had claimed that Murdock had supplied the guns and bullets, and had been paid handsomely for it. Nobody who knew the major believed it and, of course, it proved entirely false.

"Go on home now," he told us. "Get some sleep."

Sleep. I figured I could get several hours of it before I'd have to drag myself out of bed and come back. I looked at the double doors at the top of the ramp, and I wished I were someplace else. Doing just about anything else. I would have my degree from Sam Houston at the end of the summer, and I'd be free to leave the system then and get a job in the outside world. That was the plan. And I fully intended to follow it.

EXECUTION JOURNAL

Number thirteen
October 7, 1998

I first heard of Inmate Jonathan Nobles, death row inmate no. 885, weeks before his scheduled execution, when he requested to be allowed to wear a white robe for the event. My initial thought was that this wasn't too much to ask. Then I learned that he was in some way associated with the Catholic Church's Order of St. Dominic and had requested the sacrament of the Eucharist for his last meal. The more I thought about it, the more I figured I'd better keep things as normal as possible. Nobles would wear the standard execution clothing, either prison whites or "releasing clothes."

Born in 1961, he had once served a three-year stretch for theft in Collin County. He was paroled in April 1986, and returned to prison in October 16, 1987 — this time with a death sentence. Just five months after his parole, he broke into a house in Travis County and stabbed two women to death. His victims, Mitzi Johnson-Nailey and Kelly Farquhar, were twenty-one and twenty-four. Nobles, who at the time was employed by the Central Texas Crime Prevention Association, had been high on booze and drugs. Ronald Moss, Mitzi's thirty-year-old date, was also stabbed but survived. The murderer wounded himself in the arm during the bloody business, and when he was arrested at his home six days later, he made a full confession. His Diagnostic file states that he is one inch short of six feet, and weighed 202 pounds when he was processed. He weighs less than that now. His hair and eyes are brown. He's white. His file says he made it only through the eighth grade but earned a GED, compliments of the prison system and the taxpayers of Texas.

He arrives at the Walls a little before 1:30 p.m. I walk back to the death house to spend a few minutes with him.

He's hesitant about talking to me at first. Most of the men I visit with at this cell are. So I try to remember something from his file that might break the ice. I recall seeing that a hold was placed on his trust fund account in the amount of a few hundred dollars. Several years ago, he'd gone berserk and destroyed some of the prison system's television sets.

"We generally have a TV in front of this cell," I tell him. "But given your history regarding televisions, I had it removed for today."

He smiles at that, then breaks into resounding laughter — an unusual sound in this room.

He's more at ease now, and we go over his busy schedule for the rest of the afternoon. He'll receive a visit from his attorney, and another from David Deorfler with the prison system's Victim Services division. A Roman Catholic bishop is even on his list.

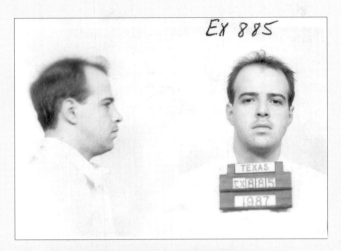

JONATHAN NOBLES, DEATH ROW INMATE NO. 885

Through the Victim/Offender Mediation and Dialogue program, Nobles recently met the mother of one of his victims, Ms. Paula Kurland. This program is relatively new in the prison system, and is quite out of the ordinary in its progressive thinking. The victim's close relative actually meets face to face with the perpetrator and confronts the inmate about the murder. It's intended to help the victim heal, as well as let the criminal understand the effect of his crime. Surprisingly, Ms. Kurland forgave Nobles for the horrible thing he had done.

"Do you plan to make a last statement?" I ask.

"Yes, sir," he says. "And I'd like to recite a Bible verse at the end of it, if that's okay. It won't be a long one."

I tell him that will be fine and go back to my office.

Later Chaplain Brazzil comes to me with two additional requests from the inmate. First, he wants to meet his executioner. The chaplain already knows my answer to this one, but he asks it anyway, since he told Nobles he would. The identity of the executioner is never revealed to the media or the witnesses, and certainly not to the condemned inmate. So, no to that one. Second, he wants to be allowed to sing "Silent Night" after he finishes his statement. This means, of course, that he will be singing as the fluids are administered.

"I guess I can't stop him," I tell the chaplain. "But I doubt he'll get very far."

Number thirteen
October 7, 1998

It's a little after six now, and I'm back at the second cell in the small row outside the execution chamber.

"Nobles," I say, "it's time for you to go into the next room with me."

I've only been doing this for seven months, and I'm sick of those words. I knew I would be, even before I said them the first time.

He makes no resistance and walks into the death chamber, where he looks at the gurney a moment before kneeling beside it and making the sign of the cross. In a matter of seconds he is on the gurney and strapped down.

We talk about his life, both before prison and on the row at the Ellis Unit. All the while, the medical people are inserting IVs and hooking up tubing. Then the needles are in, and the inmate, Chaplain Brazzil, and I are alone. It seems to take an unusually long time for the witnesses to file into the two adjacent rooms. When finally they are in place, Ms. Cockrell, the deputy director for security, steps out of the executioner's room and tells me I can proceed.

"You may make a statement if you wish," I tell Nobles.

I soon realize that we will be here longer than usual. He looks at Mrs. Kurland through the window.

"Paula, I love you, and I'm sorry," he says. "The last two weeks have been a huge blessing." I guess he's talking about their sessions. She seems touched, and even chokes up a bit. He proceeds to address each of the witnesses, both inmates' and victims', by name; he has something specific to say to each of them. Then he recites the thirteenth chapter of First Corinthians.

Tales of conversion and forgiveness, the setting of things straight and turning over of new leaves, are common here, when desperate men feel that they're about to face an accounting of a higher magnitude than the one imposed by a jury. Some of those conversions are no doubt heartfelt and sincere. Maybe this fellow's is. I don't know. What I do know is that two young women are dead because of him.

He launches into more scripture. I look at the chaplain, but he seems as confused as I am. When I've almost decided that Nobles intends to recite as much of the Bible as he can remember, he says the last line, the one he'd told me would be at the end of his statement.

I lift my glasses to signal the executioner to begin.

As promised, Nobles sings the first verse of "Silent Night," and he gets so far that I wonder whether fluid is actually moving through the IV lines. Finally, as he finishes the phrase "mother and child," the first drug puts him under.

Then it dawns on me. All the witnesses — his, the victims', and the media — will think we cut him off in the middle of his last statement. And sure enough, after the next two drugs have done their jobs and he is pronounced dead, I go up to my office and find my secretary explaining the matter to our public information director. It will be his job to explain to reporters that Nobles requested to sing his song as the drugs were being administered, not before.

I decided it wasn't a bad plan — to be singing a pretty hymn as he slipped out of one life, and into what he seemed confident was the next one.

010

AFTER CARRASCO, IT TOOK YEARS FOR THE PRISON TO return to normalcy. But years were the coin of the realm in the Walls.

After I earned my business degree from Sam Houston, I looked for work outside the prison. I glanced through the classified ads in the Houston paper occasionally. I considered a job offer in Dallas, but turned it down. I wasn't sure yet what I wanted my life's work to be, and work at the Walls would pay my bills while I decided.

My work routine was predictable, usually boring, but strangely comfortable. By this point, most of my friends worked at the Walls, and my supervisors liked me. In an odd way, I felt at home. In some ways, I'd grown as institutionalized as an old convict.

But outside of work, I was freer than I'd ever been in my life. I no longer had to study or go to classes. My future spread in front of me like an open road under clear skies. I wasn't sure where I was going, only sure that I was going somewhere.

—

SHIFTS FELL INTO WEEKS, WEEKS INTO MONTHS, AND months became years. I went before a unit board to see what might happen and was promoted to sergeant. I was happy about the promotion: No more would I have to work the pill line.

Too, the money was better — good enough that the monthly paychecks lasted almost all month before I had to begin limiting my cigarettes and beer. I shared a cheap apartment just a block from the prison with Bruce Thaler, another officer. I drove a new car, ate most of my meals in the officer's dining hall, had my laundry done by convicts, and fell into a new work schedule that gave me every other weekend off.

I stayed out till two or three o'clock most mornings. Eventually the late nights caught up with me. When I wandered in late for my 5:30 a.m. shift once too often, assistant Warden Wesley Warner told me that if it happened one more time, I'd have fifteen days to sleep as late as I wanted.

I never drew that suspension, or any other. And I was never late for work again.

In 1976, the nation turned two hundred, the Walls turned a hundred and thirty-eight, and I turned twenty-six. By then, I'd been a sergeant for long enough to have the duties down pat, but I still considered prison to be a job, not a career. I saw openings for lieutenant positions listed at other units but never applied. Then one came open at the Walls.

I applied — why not? — and got the promotion. It meant more money and more perks, like fifteen pounds of meat every month, plus milk, eggs, and cheese. In those days Texas prisons grew, raised, and made much of what their population consumed, and the overabundance spilled generously to employees of sufficient rank. The extra pay and the money we saved on groceries allowed my roommate and me to raise our partying to new heights. Bruce and I threw more than our share of informal get-togethers, drop-in affairs centered around a couple of kegs of Pearl — those courtesy not of the prison system, but of my dad, the distributor.

———

MY PROMOTION ALSO MEANT THAT I WAS ELIGIBLE FOR STATE HOUSING, BUT ONLY if I was married. So I didn't think I'd live in a prison house anytime soon.

Then one summer afternoon, about a year after I became a lieutenant, I was crossing the upper yard. Someone asked if I'd seen the new girl working in the Commission for the Blind office.

I said I hadn't.

"Well," he replied, "the view is definitely worth climbing a few stairs."

The crew that cleaned the upstairs offices every night was under my command. I decided this would be a good time to check the quality of their work.

The supervisor of the commission looked up from his desk when I stepped in. He watched as I looked into corners and wastepaper baskets, and as I ran my finger along the tops of file cabinets.

"Something we can do for you, Lieutenant?" he asked.

I said I was checking on my night crew. We chatted a bit, covering our usual subjects, and he went back to whatever he was doing. When I inspected the vicinity of the new girl's desk, the supervisor smiled. He understood my sudden diligence.

The other officer had been right: The girl was a knockout, with highlighted hair and large pretty eyes that occasionally looked up at me as I hovered. She wore a sweater — it was burnt orange — as perfectly as a human being could wear one.

The supervisor, perhaps worried that I'd hang around all afternoon, moved things forward.

"Lieutenant Willett, this is Janice Joiner. Janice, Jim Willett."

We nodded at each other. She smiled.

"You're the one who has all the parties," she said.

I said yes, that was me. And I missed a perfect opening to invite her to one. It was not the best of beginnings.

Those eyes and that sweater kept wandering into my thoughts over the next week. The next Sunday afternoon I called her and asked if she'd like to go riding around for a while. Riding around was one of the Texas preliminaries of courtship, and was particularly effective if you arrived in a handsome car. An hour later I picked her up in my pride and joy, a white Corvette.

I'd iced down some Pearl — compliments of my father — and we rode the country roads around Huntsville. Janice was easy to talk to, and she wasn't shy about carrying on her half of the conversation. I learned a lot about her that afternoon. That she'd moved around in Texas a lot as a kid, ending up in Tulsa, Oklahoma, where she'd graduated from high school. That she was working toward a degree. That she had a brother who was an officer at the Walls, who'd been her source regarding the parties. The brother had also told her that I might be a confirmed bachelor. It was true that, despite being 27 and having dated lots of girls, I'd never been serious about anyone. But I'd never found it as easy to talk with anyone as I did with Janice. I liked the way she watched me with those brown eyes, and the way she listened to me — with both keen interest and a finely tuned BS detector.

When I delivered her to her apartment, we both were convinced that we should go to dinner that night.

From that day on, I've tried not to be too far from her.

———

OUR WEDDING, A LITTLE OVER A YEAR LATER, WAS A PRISON AFFAIR FROM TOP to bottom.

Prison employees could use inmate labor by paying a "shop fee" of five bucks, plus the cost of the materials and ingredients. Inmates in the Goree Unit, the women's penitentiary on the outskirts of Huntsville, made all the flower arrangements and the wedding cakes in their vocational classes. The bridal bouquet had over two dozen roses, and the huge altar arrangement was a bursting monster of roses and gladiolas and other things that Janice could name and I couldn't. The cakes were beautiful — which met Janice's criteria — and moist — the true measure of a cake for a Texas boy raised by a good cook. The three-tiered wedding cake and chocolate groom's cake (topped with a model Corvette and the words "Get Me to the Church on Time") set us back thirty-five dollars. The reception itself was in the Goree clubhouse, which rented for twenty-five. The decorations, the cakes, the hall, and a little something for the preacher — it all cost less than a hundred bucks.

We would have been satisfied with a small church wedding with maybe some cake and punch in the fellowship hall afterwards, but my mother, being Polish, and my dad, being a beer distributor, wouldn't hear of anything less than a reception with dancing. So they provided the barbecue and the beer. Pearl, of course, frothy and ice cold from kegs. My father, though, drank his Pearl from cans kept in an ice chest in the corner. He maintained that keg beer gave him a hangover.

Captain Lindsey took a long pull on the beer in his cup and wiped the foam from his lip. "You'll have to settle down, now," he said. "And quit all your galli-vanting." He winked. "Your running-around days are done."

JIM AND JANICE WILLETT WITH A PRISON-MADE WEDDING CAKE

Major Murdock, not a beer drinker, sipped his bourbon. "From now on," he said, "you won't be running anything." He grinned.

My old roommate, Bruce Thaler, was dancing with my new one, the brand new Mrs. Jim Willett. The bottom of Janice's dress swept along the tile floor. Men took off neckties and suit coats and danced with their wives, people laughed and chattered, and a band called Fireball Express — electric guitars and keyboard, long hair, mutton chop sideburns — was sending mid-seventies tunes through large speakers that squealed at being turned up too high.

Janice looked over at me and smiled. She was beautiful, of course. Like any red-blooded American male, I was glad of that. But she was more than that. Over the last year, we had become each other's best friend, best sounding board, best everything. Looking across the room at her that night, with people laughing and talking all around us, with the screeching offerings of the band reverberating throughout the packed room, I knew that an essential aspect of my life had finally, irrevocably fallen into place.

WE SPENT THAT NIGHT IN OUR PRISON HOUSE, A SMALL TWO-STORY RESIDENCE that backed up to the Walls. The next day was a Sunday in October, which meant only one thing in the Texas prison system: the prison rodeo. For Janice and me, it meant thousands of revelers stomping under our windows on the first day of our married life. Some even picnicked on our front lawn.

ABOVE: RODEO PORTRAITS ON THE TAN STALLION

RIGHT: SUNDAY MORNING CROWD ON THE MIDWAY

HARD MONEY

The crowds gathered early on rodeo mornings, long before the event itself started at two. The midway opened at eight thirty, and folks milled around long before that. The prison-run midway offered loads of food and drink concessions, a booth that would print your picture on a wanted poster, and a life-sized plastic stallion, rearing on its hind legs as it had for decades, while generations of children climbed on for photos. Everywhere you could hear the constant, clipped cadence of a precision drill team made up of inmates from the Retrieve Unit. The sound mixed with the songs from convict country-and-western bands that took their turns on a stage. The area on 12th Street looked more like a county fair than the front of a prison.

One of the three main gates to the rodeo arena lay between our house and the east wall, and multitudes stood in line only a few feet from our dining room window. Bored, they often leaned forward and stood on tiptoes to get a better view. Janice learned to stay clear of the windows.

The rodeo was the brainchild of Lee Simmons, the head of the Texas prison system in 1931. Simmons figured a rodeo would provide much-needed entertainment for the townspeople, then mired in the Depression, and for the inmates, depressed for an altogether different reason. Over the years, the event grew into a Texas tradition, and the huge arena was constructed where a baseball field had once stood. By the time Janice and I woke up to that early-morning commotion outside our windows, the rodeo drew close to a hundred thousand spectators each October, and prisoners from every Texas penitentiary were bused to the arena, where they sat in a gigantic section of bleachers surrounded by high metal fences topped with barbed wire.

Except for the female barrel racers, convicts were the only participants in the rodeo. They rode bareback, and they rode broncs and bulls. In the calf scramble, a group competed against each other to tie calves and drag them into a ring. They even raced chariots, as fast and furious as the race in Ben Hur. But by far the most popular event was something called Hard Money, when a mean, aggravated bull was released into the arena with forty red-shirted inmates. Tied to the bull's horns was a Bull Durham tobacco sack. Each of the forty red-shirts aimed to end up with the sack, which always contained at least fifty dollars, but often as much as fifteen hundred after local patrons added to the stash. The one who finally lifted the sack to the judge was often a bloody spectacle.

RETRIEVE UNIT INMATE DRILL TEAM

RODEO CLOWNS

Each event featured a performance by a professional entertainer, and the list of stars who worked the rodeo read like a Who's Who of country-music legends: Eddie Arnold, Johnny Cash, Ernest Tubb, Dolly Parton, Johnny Rodriguez, Willie Nelson, and Tom. T. Hall. Even John Wayne did a turn. He didn't have to do anything to please the roaring crowd except stand there and be John Wayne.

One Sunday, a young singer named Tanya Tucker refused to go onstage in the rain — never mind that thousands in the stands had sat through that rain for the entire first half of the rodeo. Mr. Estelle, who was the director at the time, offered to let her sing from the enclosed media booth, but that idea didn't appeal to her. Legend has it that at that point, Mr. Estelle, who was not used to dealing with prima donnas, told her to remove her things from her dressing-room trailer and hit the road. She demanded a ride to the airport. He mentioned something about a taxi.

The day after my wedding, my 2 p.m.-till-10 shift required me to oversee the inside of the unit while everyone else was at the rodeo. During the performance,

PREVIOUS PAGES: VIEW OF ARENA

CHAPTER TEN

I didn't have much to do, but once it was over, things went into high gear. All the Walls inmates who had attended the show had to be counted back into the unit and fed their supper. And the hundreds who had been bused from other units throughout the system had to be removed from the secured area of the arena, kept in the exact order in which they were brought in, moved to the back gate, searched, and then counted onto the buses. Once they were all tallied and back on the road, it was time to rack up the entire Walls population and get a count. By the end, I was exhausted.

Janice and I decided not to attend the big party that came at the end of the last rodeo of the year. It was the first end-of-the-rodeo party I'd missed since I began working in the prison. But I didn't at all mind spending the evening with Janice, in the little house beside the Walls.

011

THE STATE PHONE IN OUR DUPLEX RANG — A REVER-
berating long ring that nearly always meant trouble.
Janice sighed and put her purse down. Anytime that
line rang, something was wrong, and I was needed
somewhere neither of us wanted me to be.

It was a warm Saturday afternoon in early April.
I was a lieutenant, Janice was six months pregnant,
and we were getting dressed to head downtown and
see a movie.

Captain Pritchett's voice had its usual military
precision, but this time it betrayed a sense of urgency:
"Get in your uniform and get to the east gate as soon
as possible. Call me in the warden's office when you
get there."

I changed into my gray uniform, kissed Janice
goodbye, and double-timed it through the empty rodeo
arena, across the back parking lot, and to the east gate
office. I called the warden's number.

Captain Pritchett answered on the first ring. "A
van will be arriving at the east gate shortly," he said.
"From Ellis. They'll have a convict in back that's
been shot." He spoke slowly and precisely, as always,
careful to let his orders sink in.

"Get on board and show the driver how to get to
the hospital," he continued. "When you get there,
take custody of that inmate." Another pause. In my
mind's eye I could see the captain leaning forward

over the phone. "And, Jim, you ask him why he shot himself. Understand?"

As I put the receiver down, I wondered how a prisoner had come to possess a firearm. I didn't get to wonder long; the van soon bounced to a halt at the sallyport. I got in with the two Ellis officers and pointed straight ahead of us — down the driveway bordered by the boiler house and the textile mill, on one side, the mechanical department on the other; past the old tag plant; behind the print shop; and into the narrow lane between the end of Five Building and the west wall. We headed across the upper yard and pulled in front of the three-story white hospital.

I got out and took my first look at Eroy Brown, a black inmate of average height, and the cause of the current excitement. He'd been quiet while we drove.

The convict hobbled into the hospital. In the hallway, at the desk where an officer was keeping watch, I called Captain Pritchett to say that we'd arrived.

As we walked down the hall, I asked Brown why he'd shot himself. He didn't answer, so I asked again.

"I didn't shoot myself," he said.

A male nurse and his inmate assistant were soon tending to a gunshot wound on Brown's foot. Someone was playing KSAM, the Huntsville radio station. The disc jockey interrupted the country music with a bulletin — an event rare enough in itself to make me take notice. Legend had it that on a long-ago November day, the station had waited to finish a long commercial for Goolsby Drugs before reporting that President Kennedy had been shot.

We all listened as the announcer read the words too fast; they stumbled over each other. There had been an incident at the Ellis Unit, he said. People had been shot; the warden was one of them. An inmate had also been wounded and transferred to the Walls hospital.

The male nurse, his assistant and I were all suddenly aware what had happened and who we had with us.

Warden Pursley and Captain Pritchett joined us in the room. It was quiet as a funeral.

The nurse dug out the bullet, plinked it into a steel bowl. He marked it so that he could recognize it later, as evidence, and Warden Pursley took possession of it.

The nurse began to clean the wound. I stared at Brown, laid out on the examination table. Too often, as ordinary days, weeks and months rolled by at the

Walls, those of us in the gray uniforms forgot that in prison, things could turn deadly fast. He looked scared, and I wasn't surprised when he was placed on suicide watch.

Later, I learned more of the sad story. In the Ellis farm shop, farm manager Billy Moore had a problem with inmate Brown — a problem serious enough that Moore called the warden for help. The two men attempted to handcuff Brown, who somehow grabbed Pack's pistol. In the scuffle, Brown apparently shot and killed Moore, then overtook Warden Pack and drowned him in the nearby creek. How the prisoner himself came to be shot remained a mystery.

When Brown's trial came to court, I sat in the gallery with other prison employees, all of us there on our own time. When Brown was acquitted of murder charges, the verdict hit us like a kick in the stomach. We were numb. We'd watched justice lurch horribly awry, and we were angry.

Not long after the trial, Brown was paroled. It didn't take him long to commit another crime serious enough to land him back in our care, but this time he howled about fearing for his life, given the certain animosity of his keepers. He ended up in a federal penitentiary outside of Texas.

———

THE GUARD IN THE NUMBER FOUR PICKET WAVED DOWN AT ME AND PULLED THE collar of his uniform jacket tight against his neck with his free hand — the one that wasn't holding a shotgun.

"Mighty cold one, Captain," he called. I nodded in his direction, allowing that it was. It was less than an hour till midnight, and a damp, heavy chill had settled over east Texas. Tomorrow would be December 7, Pearl Harbor Day 1982, but at the Walls, that wasn't the significant thing about the date.

The Supreme Court had lifted the moratorium on capital punishment, and Texas was ready to resume executions. I couldn't have answered many questions about Charley Brooks, who was about to become the first inmate executed by lethal injection. Neither could I have offered much in the way of a personal philosophy regarding the death penalty. Until then, I hadn't worried about the rightness or wrongness of capital punishment. Until then, it wasn't something that we did at the Walls.

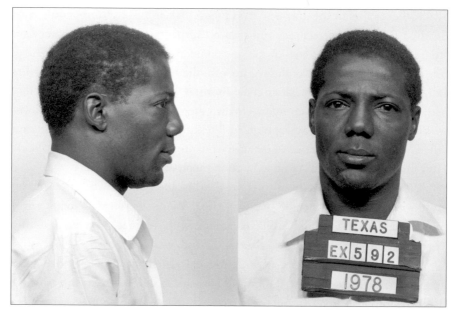

CHARLEY BROOKS, DEATH ROW INMATE NO. 592

The guard in the picket stretched up on his toes to see the front of the unit. "Awful lot of people out there," he called down. "I keep hearing 'em." His words turned into small clouds of vapor. "All them TV lights keep going on and off up there. At first I thought it was lightning."

In the early afternoon the media vans and cars had descended, all wedged as close to the Walls as was allowed. Miles of cables snaked along sidewalks and streets; awkwardly shaped antennae poked up into the cold, gray afternoon, then later, into the colder night. In spite of the weather, a crowd of spectators began forming early, some in hunting gear, others in tattered denim with peace symbols that had survived the seventies. Many of the men had shaved necks; some had ponytails. A few people brought their small children, who were wrapped in blankets and either stood beside their parents or sat on the curbs. Some people had cameras; most had opinions. Loud Sam Houston State students waved signs supporting the execution. Others, just as loud, held signs opposing it. Handmade signs quoted the Bible. Both death-penalty advocates and opponents had found plenty of scripture to justify their positions.

Some of the crowd, though, didn't seem to have an opinion one way or another — at least not one strong enough to warrant standing outside on a frigid night. They'd wandered up, drawn by commotion and the undeniable appeal of a big, out-of-the-ordinary event in a quiet Piney Woods town. The execution attracted them as if it were a burning house or a car wreck.

The protesters gathered in front of the prison, where they'd be visible to the media; regular spectators gathered on the lawn beside the administration building and along Avenue I, down the hill beside the director's mansion and the big cotton warehouse and the western wall. Someone who came in later, when the horde had swollen even larger, told me that it seemed evenly divided between those in favor and those opposed. The Huntsville police department was out in force, along with deputies from the Walker County sheriff's office, local constables, Highway Patrol troopers, and even a few Texas Rangers, who towered over anyone they stood beside. Looming height and bulk seemed to be requirements for the job.

A helicopter frump, frump, frumped over the east wall, its bright lights digging into the darkness.

"They's three of 'em", the guard yelled down when the chopper had moved far enough away that I could hear him. "Channel 13, Channel 2, and Channel 11, I think." He looked as another approached loudly from the direction of the university; he pointed at it with the barrel of his shotgun.

"I just hope they don't run into one another," he shouted.

AFTER THE EAST GATE OFFICER CHECKED THE HEARSE, I GOT IN THE FRONT SEAT, beside Mr. King from the Huntsville Funeral Home, and gave him directions. We traced the same circuitous route that Eroy Brown had traveled twenty months before.

When we got to the death house, I showed Mr. King exactly where the hearse should go.

"We're supposed to just wait, now," I said. Mr. King nodded, and turned off the engine. The other man from the funeral home twisted around to get a better view of the building.

"It's not as big as I thought," he said.

We watched as prison employees in suits entered, followed by men holding notebooks.

"Those are reporters," I said. "Warden Pursley said that they would watch the whole procedure, then give a report outside. And answer questions."

The warden had worked for months, preparing for tonight. The Supreme Court had reversed its view on capital punishment in 1972, and several states had already carried out executions. Prison officials had long known that it was only a matter of time before Texas would do the same.

In the mid-seventies Warden Husbands instructed Jack Pursley, the mechanical supervisor at the Walls, to make the old electric chair serviceable again. Pursley's crew checked the connections and made new restraining straps, but to no avail. The Texas Legislature then decreed that death row inmates would henceforth be dispatched by lethal injection. So Old Sparky was unbolted from the floor, and the fat wires disconnected. The big chair, with its dangling straps and electrodes still attached, was dragged to the end of the cellblock. Nobody knew what else to do with it. And there it sat, in a crate specially built for it.

By the time one Charley Brooks reached the end of his appeals, it was 1982, a full decade after the court had reversed itself on capital punishment. Jack Pursley, who had refurbished the electric chair only to put it into storage, was now the senior warden of the Walls. It fell to him to carry out the legislature's will.

I looked at my watch. Less than thirty minutes till midnight. Then I looked at the death house. A man locked in one of its eight cells was about to become an unwilling pioneer.

In 1976, at a car lot in Tarrant County, Charley Brooks had asked to test-drive a car. A mechanic went with him. A few blocks away Brooks stopped to pick up a buddy (thereafter referred to as "the co-defendant"), and the two men forced the mechanic into the trunk. They drove to a motel, took the mechanic into a room, bound him with wire coat hangers, gagged him with tape, and shot him in the head. Then they made off with the new car.

In the late sixties Brooks had done time in the federal pen at Leavenworth, Kansas, for illegal possession of firearms. Before that, he spent a short stay in the Texas prison system. In 1978 he came home for good as death row inmate no. 592.

He'd arrived at the Walls in a van from the Ellis Unit at seven a.m. — almost seventeen hours ago — and was placed a cell in the block next to the execution chamber. He wanted oysters and shrimp for his last supper, but had been given steak and fries since the rule was that meals, even that last one, had to consist of items on hand in the prison kitchen. He was forty years old, black, one inch short of six feet tall, and weighed one hundred and fifty pounds. In about fifteen minutes, he would become the first inmate Texas had executed in almost twenty years, and the first in the entire United States to be put to death by lethal injection.

For weeks, Warden Pursley had made sure that everyone knew exactly where they were supposed to be and what they were supposed to do. We ran mock drills, with officers playing everyone from the executioner to the condemned man. I was assigned to guide the hearse into the Walls, keep it secure inside the unit, and escort it, with Brooks' body on board, back to the east gate and off the premises.

For a long few moments Mr. King, his assistant, and I watched people go in and out of the small, red-brick building. At midnight, nobody came or went at all. I could only imagine what was happening inside.

I took another stab at forming my own opinion. I knew that Charley Brooks had committed a horrible crime. But I also knew that he was alive and was — right this very minute — being made dead.

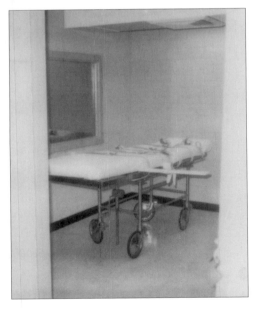

EARLY LETHAL INJECTION GURNEY

The only thing I was sure of was that I was damned glad to not be in there. I figured that I could go the rest of my life without watching someone die, even someone who well deserved it.

It got cold in the hearse. Mr. King turned the key in the ignition and nudged the heater button.

The man behind me turned again to look at the closed door.

"If this hasn't never been done before," he said, leaning closer behind me, "how does anybody know that stuff's gonna work?"

Mr. King and I looked out the window at the death house. The bright television lights spilled over the top of the walls. We could hear what must have been several hundred people. One group was chanting; another was singing a hymn. I couldn't make out the words. A helicopter churned close by. It was as if the whole world had congregated outside the walls or was floating over them.

Mr. King looked straight ahead through the windshield.

"It better work," he said.

■ ■

IT DID.

Charlie Brooks made a long statement laced with his confidence in Allah, received the triple dose, and died.

We were signaled to enter. I accompanied Mr. King and his assistant only as far as the door to the death house. They rolled a gurney in and came back out almost immediately with the draped body. I watched them collapse the legs of the gurney and slide it into the back of the hearse. We drove slowly to the back of the unit. This time nobody said anything. We looked straight ahead, all too conscious of the new addition to our company.

When we reached the sallyport, I said goodnight, got out, and watched as the east gate officer pushed his rolling mirror under the vehicle, looked into the windows, and tapped his hand against the side. The heavy gate slid open, and the hearse slipped out into the cold night. A highway patrol car moved in front of it, red lights flashing, and the gate closed behind it.

I shivered, telling myself it was the damp and chill. I pushed my hands deep into the pockets of my jacket.

So, I thought as I walked away, we're killing people now. I'd never counted on that. Though I'd known it was a possibility — even a probability — for almost all of my eleven years here. Now, though, it was a fact.

I didn't know this man whose body I'd guided out the east gate. I'd never heard of him until a few weeks before. It was easy to be ambivalent about Charley Brooks.

I felt differently about Eroy Brown, whose confident smirk had held my gaze in the courtroom, whose victims I had respected and mourned. Maybe, I thought, people's attitudes regarding capital punishment only hold together until they're affected personally. Maybe, I thought, ways of looking at things break down when you move from general to specific.

I didn't know. But I did know that things had suddenly changed in the Walls.

012

WE ALL KNEW THE STORY OF HOW PAUL HAYMES MADE
quite a first impression at the Texas Department of
Criminal Justice. The former FBI agent had been hired
to head a new department called Operational Audits,
the equivalent of a police department's internal-affairs
unit. When Mr. Estelle, the director, introduced the
new employee at a wardens' meeting, Mr. Haymes stood
up, beamed a smile as broad as his fire-engine-red
necktie, and said he was happy as a man with two
dicks, to be aboard.

The big room fell quiet, and — except for Mr.
Estelle — everyone looked down at the table. The
director looked dourly at Haymes, then at two female
wardens sitting in the back.

Mr. Haymes continued as he'd begun: with vigor,
and not making any friends along the way. Of course,
in his position — as resident bloodhound tracking
internal mistakes and malfeasance — he didn't
expect to make friends.

He came looking for me one May morning, and
offered me a job with his unit. He didn't say why he
thought I'd be good at it, or who'd recommended me
to him. He just brusquely said he wanted me. I turned
him down flat.

Then things changed. In June, Warden Pursley
called me in to tell me Janice had just telephoned:
My father had died. The warden had liked my dad,

and had given him a personal, lengthy tour of the Walls one October Sunday morning before the rodeo. Everyone back home at Groesbeck had heard about that tour — probably more often and at greater length than they'd cared to — and whenever Dad came to Huntsville, he brought the warden a case of Pearl. For a man like Jack Pursley, the gift was a double boon: It was beer, and it was free.

The warden came to the funeral, along with several others from the Walls. We buried my father beside his mother, who I'd loved like sunshine and air. It was more than a little difficult to stand in that country cemetery looking down at the pair of graves, side by side, that represented two missing pieces in my life.

In the weeks that followed, I thought hard about fathers and sons. My own son, Jacob, was nearly two and I didn't see nearly enough of him. Much of the time, he was asleep when I was awake, or he was awake when I was at work. Something needed to change.

A job in Operational Audits would mean that I worked eight to five, Monday through Friday, for the first time in my career, and could count on taking weekends and holidays off. I could leave on vacations; staffing shortage meant that I hadn't had one in years. It would also mean a promotion to major, and the extra money would allow Janice and me to buy a house of our own, one not owned by the state and in the shadow of a prison.

Perhaps most persuasive, the job offered a chance to work in an area other than security. Keeping prisoners in prison had become significantly harder since 1980, when a federal judge, in his Ruiz v. Estelle ruling, required enormous changes in the way Texas ran its prisons. No longer could a warden use "building tenders," inmates who oversaw and carried out countless routine day-to-day operations. The old system had worked well for longer than anyone could remember, but now already overworked officers had to carry out duties once performed by building tenders.

But I still had one reservation about the job. When Mr. Haymes told me the offer was still good, I asked specifically if I would ever have to investigate prison personnel. He assured me that I would not, that my assignment would be strictly to make sure the units complied with the Support Service Inmate section of the Ruiz ruling. SSI was the court-ordered replacement for the building tender system, and I would check to see that a particular inmate was eligible to work a particular job, and that he was not being made to exercise authority over other inmates.

That shouldn't ruffle my friends' feathers, I figured. Janice and I talked over the decision. Then we packed my gray uniforms away and bought neckties, dress shirts and slacks — a new wardrobe for a new job.

BURNED-UP CORNFIELDS AND LITTLE TRICKLES OF CREEKS SLID OUTSIDE THE windows of the car from the motor pool. The big digital thermometer on a Huntsville bank had reported eighty-six degrees as we'd left town, and that was at half past six in the morning. By the time we'd turned off Interstate 45 at Buffalo and headed northeast, the late summer sun had climbed high enough into the East Texas sky to push the temperature into the mid-nineties. The heavy, boat-like Dodge wasn't fancy, was a tad out of alignment, and wasn't much to look at, but it zipped along. And the air conditioner worked.

For most of the hour that we'd been on the road, Mr. Haymes sat quietly on the passenger side of the wide front seat, watching one parched pasture dotted with sedentary, skeletal cattle after another. One stand of thirsty pines and oaks after another. The day before, he'd dropped by my office and said he'd heard I would be driving to the Coffield Unit this morning. He asked if he could tag along. Had a little digging to do up there, he said. For the director. No use, he figured, on wasting gas when we were both going to the same place.

As the car climbed gradually out of the Keechi Creek bottom toward Oakwood on Highway 79, he asked what I had on my agenda this morning.

"Just routine SSI audits at Coffield and Beto," I said.

He nodded and looked back out the window.

"I'd just as soon trade with you today," he said.

He didn't say why. I didn't ask. Since I'd gone to work for him four months before, our relationship had been strictly professional: boss and employee. He was in his mid-fifties — at least twenty years my senior — and his lean, square-jawed face never exuded friendship, at least not in my direction.

Not until we turned off of the highway onto the little road that led to Tennessee Colony did Mr. Haymes reveal the purpose of his trip. During a recent escape attempt at the Coffield Unit, a convict working in the fields had made a run for it and been captured shortly thereafter. Someone reported that, when the officer who had captured him radioed the unit, Warden Bob Cousins replied, "Do something to his ass." This order, whether it had been carried out or not, would constitute a direct, flagrant violation of the Ruiz mandate known as the Use of Force Plan. To put it simply, if a prison employee put his hand on an inmate, he'd damned well better be doing one of two things: stopping an escape or defending himself. Since the Coffield escapee had already been captured, neither of these could have been the case. And with intense scrutiny coming from the court and the media, Mr. Estelle wanted the matter investigated and cleared up.

We were quiet for the rest of the trip. It was clear that Mr. Estelle wanted nothing more than for Haymes to prove that this thing had not, in fact, happened. Warden Cousins had been with the prison system for many years and was well thought of.

At Coffield, we showed the guard our identification cards and were cleared to enter the compound. Nobody was overjoyed to see us, but we were used to that. The reason for the chief's trip to Coffield had no doubt worked its way through the grapevine.

I was shown to a room where I spent the next couple of hours reading files and interviewing convicts. Then I waited a few minutes up front for Mr. Haymes to come out of Warden Cousin's office. They stepped out together, shook hands, and seemed friendly. Well and good, I thought.

From there, we drove to the nearby Beto Unit — named for "Walking George," the immune-to-tear-gas director — and Mr. Haymes, obviously relieved, told me that all had gone nicely at Coffield. He had interviewed everyone in possession of a radio on the day of the escape, and no one had heard any such order from the warden. He leaned back in the seat and sighed, obviously happy.

At Beto, we spent an hour or so doing exactly the same thing we'd done at Coffield. Then we ate lunch at the unit and headed home.

Mr. Haymes had sunk into a quiet, frowning mood. Probably sleepy, I thought. We'd had pork roast, fresh turnip greens, and cornbread for lunch, and I certainly could have used a nap.

He took off his glasses and rubbed his eyes before closing them tight. He stayed quiet a long time before shaking his head slowly. When he started talking, I realized that he wasn't speaking to me as much as to himself. I just happened to be the only other human being in the car.

"I asked the same questions at Beto that I did at Coffield," he said, keeping his gaze locked on the highway in front of us. "And nearly every last man that had a radio that day swore that Cousins said it."

He put his glasses back on and didn't say anything else all the way to Huntsville.

Mr. Estelle himself visited Warden Cousins a few weeks later. It was a show of personal respect, since the hatchet jobs usually fell to Bobby Maggard, the deputy director. Nobody, at least at my level, knew whether Cousins had been allowed to resign or was fired. But he was gone.

Such was the nature of my new job.

___

AS SUMMER TURNED TO FALL, THE SPECIAL MASTER APPOINTED TO OVERSEE THE prison system's compliance with the Ruiz mandates began calling for more investigations than Mr. Haymes and his handful of investigators could handle, especially since the Special Master had broadened the scope of the allegations to include some prior to the implementation of the Ruiz decrees. Haymes told everyone in the department that, in addition to our SSI cases, we would each be assigned files involving prison personnel. Which was exactly what I had been told I wouldn't have to do. Exactly what I had no desire to do.

I had become the enemy. I knew it, and everybody out on the units knew it. Us vs. them: It felt as if we had chosen up sides, and I knew that more than a few of my friends thought I was on the wrong one.

The first case I drew was again from Coffield, where an inmate accused the new warden of kicking him. I prayed on the drive there that the case would be open-and-shut, that the convict was out-and-out lying.

The warden made no bones about considering this case to be bullshit. He categorically denied the charge and had several inmates lined up as witnesses to substantiate his story. Unfortunately, each one worked directly for him at an SSI job, which meant that they'd hit upon an air-conditioned, relatively pleasant way to serve a stretch in the pen. Keeping those jobs, I figured on the way back to Huntsville, could motivate a little fabrication — or a lot.

I made another trip to Coffield to ask more questions, and still found nothing conclusive. Mr. Haymes decided to make our first use of a tool recently allowed by the Ruiz Special Master. On my third trip north, I went to the warden's office to tell him we'd be giving the inmate a lie detector test. The warden gave me a piece of his mind, and I tried explaining that if the inmate failed, the case would be closed. It didn't help. When I left his office, his face and neck were a noticeably darker shade of red.

A week later the inmate was taken to Austin and given a polygraph exam. The test said that he was being deceptive, and the case was closed.

So 1983 drew to an end. The Operational Audits job had its benefits, and I enjoyed them. With the extra pay, Janice and I bought a nice place out in the country, and I had every weekend and evening off to be with her and Jacob, who was now a frantic bundle of two-year-old energy. And though I loathed the investigations I hadn't been forced to investigate a friend.

At least not yet.

IN THE FIRST MONTHS OF THE NEW YEAR, THE SPECIAL MASTER'S OFFICE LEANED on us hard to clear up files that had been open for a while. Mr. Haymes was gone now, and his assistant Keith Price was the interim chief. One morning, Keith threw a file on my desk and told me it couldn't wait until the investigator who had started it came back from vacation. I'd have to do it.

Keith stayed in the doorway long enough for me to look up at him.

"You're not going to like this one, Jim," he said. Then he went back down the hall.

When he was gone, I leaned back in my chair and began scanning. It was a "use of force" case — no surprise there; they all were — regarding an incident that was two years old. I didn't have to read much further before seeing the name that made me stop short and sit upright in my chair. I read it again to make sure. Then my heart sank.

Kent Ramsey.

He'd come to the Walls from the Diagnostic Unit a few years previously, when he'd been promoted to lieutenant. Both his parents had worked for the prison system, and Kent grew up on prison property, in prison housing, and had gone to work for the system immediately after graduating from high school. In his entire life, he had never lived anywhere but Texas prisons. He'd been a captain for a while at the Walls, and our association had evolved into friendship. Pretty much everyone who knew him or worked with him would have agreed that he was one of the bright ones, an up-and-comer. He was presently the warden at a unit that, coincidently, shared his name: Ramsey II.

As I'd expected, Kent wasn't any happier with the fact that I'd be conducting the investigation than I was. In fact, he hated the prospect of being investigated at all for something that had happened so long ago. Our interviews were cordial and professional, but completely void of the banter and kidding we'd once enjoyed. The facts of the case were simple: A building tender had been killed when Kent had been at Ellis, and the convict who'd killed him had later been injured. I interviewed inmates and prison personnel, backtracked through testimonies and records, and reached the one conclusion that I hoped to avoid: Kent must have had at least some knowledge of how the inmate came to be injured — knowledge that never ended up in a report or a file.

I fretted for several days. I lost sleep. I stewed. Prayed.

Then I did my job.

The report I filed resulted in Kent Ramsey's being relieved as a senior warden and transferred to a desk job in Huntsville. Now he seemed destined for a career altogether different from the one that he (and everybody else) had felt sure lay in store for him. I couldn't shake the nagging feeling that I had been the cause of his downfall.

My only consolation was the belief that had someone else been given the case — someone less interested in either Kent or the absolute truth — Kent might very well have been fired outright. In fact, the Special Master's office had wanted him terminated, but Red McKaskle, Mr. Estelle's successor as director, had disregarded their advice and opted for reassignment. I'd heard the bluster from a few of my coworkers and knew that Kent's head would have been an impressive addition to their trophy wall. I was certain that the Special Master's office had targeted specific people to bring down, and I was just as certain that Kent Ramsey was on their hit list. Why else would they have dredged up a two-year-old file that was as cold as a Texas norther?

The Ramsey case left me certain of two things.

I liked my job even less than I had before.

And I wanted out.

MY NEXT FILE CAME FROM ELLIS, WHICH WAS TURNING OUT TO BE A CONSTANT performer in this circus.

It was another old case, this time concerning a convict who had been abused in the inmate barbershop. A supervisor had been terminated because of the incident, but somebody in the Special Master's office had gotten wind that another officer had been present when it occurred. The abused inmate was still at Ellis.

The captain who showed me to Ellis's interview room returned a few minutes later with an old convict, who took a seat. When the captain had gone and closed the door, I got to the point, hoping to be back at the Walls for lunch. I said I needed to talk to him about the barber shop incident, and needed to know whether the officer being investigated was in the room during the assault.

The inmate looked down at the table for a moment, inspected his finger-nails, then leaned forward.

He looked around to make sure the door was closed. He spoke slowly, as if he had all the time in the world. "The guilty man done been took care of this time, Boss." He nodded. Winked. "This here's done."

He leaned even further toward me. "No second man wasn't never in that barbershop," he said. "There wasn't nobody in there 'cepting that sumbitch what hit me. And that's a fact."

I'd learned a thing or two about prisoners, and I could almost always tell when one was lying. This one was lying.

There is a code among inmates that have been locked up for any extended length of time. It's a strong code, one that involves many things including loyalty not only to other convicts that they feel are worthy of it, but to certain guards as well. It was that code that made some of the building tenders look after me when I had been a new boot, to tell when it was "time to roll the doors now, Boss," and to go into a row and make a cantankerous inmate turn his radio down when I'd already told him to do it. And it was that code that drove this man sitting across the table from me to protect an officer who I felt sure had been in attendance when another one had, in prison lingo, "touched this convict up a little."

"You sure about that?" I asked.

"Yes, sir."

CHAPTER TWELVE

I fished a pen out of my pocket, and tore a sheet of yellow paper off my pad. "Will you write that down here and sign it?"

He did.

With that signature the case was closed. The Special Master's office was surprised by the outcome, but I wasn't. Nobody in the Special Master's office had spent as much time as I had in a prison.

By midsummer, when I'd had about all I could take, I was rescued by Bobby Maggard, the former assistant director who had become even less popular, if that was possible, than the rest of us who worked in Operational Audits. His job was to bring to closure the cases — and in most cases the careers — of personnel who had been determined to be guilty. On many of these trips he used the system's airplane to travel to the unit where the deed had to be done. His jaunts had become so common that guards in the pickets who saw the light plane approach would mimic the catch phrase from Fantasy Island: "De plane, de plane."

It turned out that Bobby Maggard was as sick of his job as I was of mine. He was sitting in one of the chairs in Warden Pursley's office one morning when I'd been asked to come downstairs.

"Bobby wants to talk to you," the warden said, then walked out and closed the door behind him.

Mr. Maggard cut directly to the chase. He had just been named the warden at Pack II, a unit in Navasota, a hour west of Huntsville. He needed an assistant warden and Warden Pursley had recommended me. Did I want the job?

"Can I talk it over with my wife?" I asked him.

He shook his head. Looked at his watch.

"I need to know right now," he said.

So I took a deep breath, and said the handful of words that allowed me to leave Operational Audits forever.

It had been almost exactly a full calendar year since I'd gone to work for Mr. Haymes. It wasn't the most enjoyable of years, to say the least, and opinions might vary as to whether it was a productive one. But it was soon to be over, and I'd be returning to the job I'd always done in the system.

Though I hadn't liked the year I'd spent in operational audits, I was satisfied that I'd done a good job there. I'd been fair.

Whenever I found myself sitting in judgment of anyone who had been charged, I always remembered a scene from my own life.

One of our investigators was working on a case that came from the Wynne Unit. Back in 1982, a couple of convicts had escaped one evening and were captured late that night not far away. The inmates maintained that they had been burned with a lit cigarette during questioning back at the unit. John Gilbert, the investigator, pursued the case even after one of the inmates failed a polygraph, when the file could have been officially closed. Finally, a guard contacted the investigators and spilled his guts. Several officers were fired, and some did some time in federal prison. The investigator had done thorough work this time, and everyone knew it.

What everyone didn't know was that on that night in 1982, when I'd been a captain, Jerry Peterson, the assistant warden at the Walls, had called me to go on that manhunt with him. We'd driven the back roads for hours until the message came over the radio that the inmates had been captured and were being returned to the unit. Back at Wynne, I parked outside the back gate, and Warden Peterson said maybe we'd better go in to see if we could help with the investigation. Then he looked at his watch, yawned, and decided they probably didn't need us. We went home.

Who's to say what would have happened if I had been in there that night? I certainly would never have burned a man with a cigarette. That much I was sure of. But I might have ended up as a witness facing a very real moral dilemma about testifying against a fellow officer.

My long year in Operational Audits helped me to see situations through someone else's eyes, something I'd tried to do with inmates ever since I'd been a new boot. I learned how to get to the root causes and eventual solutions of problems, a skill that would serve me well during the remainder of my career. And, of course, I was one rung higher on the pay scale.

Those were the things I took away from that year.

But whenever I thought of Kent Ramsey, a good man and a good friend, I never felt that I'd gained more than I lost.

013

EVERY STAR IN THE HEAVENS SEEMED TO HAVE CONGRE-
gated directly over the prison farm to watch the old
year slip away and the new one take its place. It was
one of those clear, still Texas winter nights warm
enough to go outside to look at the stars but chilly
enough to discourage lingering with them.

I was the duty officer this weekend. One of an
assistant warden's unofficial functions was to take duties
that the senior warden didn't want, like having to abstain
from drinking on New Year's Eve. I was alone in the
assistant warden's residence across the road from the
unit; I spent a lot of time alone there. When we'd moved
to Navasota for my job with Pack II, Janice had gone to
work for the parole office in the unit. Four years later,
I was told that I would be assigned to one of the Huntsville
units soon, so we thought it prudent for Janice to put in
for a transfer. Hers was approved promptly; two years
later, I was still an hour away from Huntsville and my
family. So much for prudence. She and the kids
moved back to Huntsville, to the country place we'd
lived in before. I stayed here during the work week
and on the weekends, like this one, when I had to stay
close to the prison.

Earlier that night, I talked on the phone with Janice
and Jacob and his little sister Jordan, then clicked
through the TV channels long enough to determine
that nothing interested me. For a while I worked on a

Southern Pacific locomotive that was a new addition to my train collection. Then I stared out the window, felt sorry for myself, and looked at my watch to see that it was a quarter till midnight. I decided that one beer wouldn't be such a bad thing on a totally uneventful Sunday night.

I grabbed a cold one out of the fridge and walked out to the back yard, with all those stars. They shone over the little community of Courtney, dark and quiet and made up of fewer human beings than were locked up in the prison beside it. They shone over the prison farm itself, and the rich blackland pastures that spread to the edge of the bluffs overlooking the Brazos River.

At exactly midnight I hoisted my beer to the arrival of 1990 and, since it was a Pearl, to my father, gone now for seven years. A few fireworks slowly climbed over Courtney and burst into colorful explosions, joined a few seconds later by more over the prison-employee residence area, then by the distant popping of gunshots from all directions. Country folk liked to fire rifles, pistols, and sometimes even shotguns into the night sky on New Year's Eve.

I finished the beer, hoping that Janice had let Jacob stay up late enough to watch fireworks in Huntsville. He was eight now, and had lived most of those years at Pack II, often under the watchful gaze of Donald Walker, a young inmate who I had assigned to be the groundskeeper at our duplex. Walker did everything from play catch with Jacob to serve as lifeguard at the above-ground pool in our backyard. I realized that Jacob needed a guardian when he was about four. That day a picket officer called, wanting to know if I had a little boy. I said yes, and asked him why.

"Because," he'd said, "he's about halfway up the fence here beside my picket."

I walked Jacob back across the bridge, and Janice nearly smothered him in a bear hug. When she'd heard the bloodhounds baying at the dog kennel, she panicked, terrified that her baby had wandered into one of the pens.

The pyrotechnics and small artillery fire had spent themselves, and the stars had the wide sky all to themselves again. I went in to get ready for bed. As I was walking through the hallway to the bedroom, the state phone rang.

"Warden Willett," said the lieutenant on the other end of the line, "we've got a little problem here."

JACOB WILLETT WITH INMATE DONALD WALKER

In the background, I could hear a commotion. I asked what was going on.

"The inmates are rowdy, sir," he said. A long moment passed. "They aren't following orders to go to their bunks," he finally said.

"You go down there yourself," I told him. "You tell them to rack up. Right now! And call me back when you're done."

I sat down in the living room to wait for his call.

This was a new breed of inmates for me. Until Pack II, I had spent my entire career at the Walls, where the convicts were mostly old men. At the end of their day, they were tired and wanted to go to bed. Pack II was a juvenile population, ages seventeen to twenty-one, and these kids had as much energy at midnight as they had before breakfast. Not one of them had ever heard of older convicts' code regarding respect for each other and for any officers that they felt deserved it. Most of these younger inmates respected nothing and no one, least of all any of us who were in charge of them. That lack of respect manifested itself — daily, hourly, and every second of every minute — in a blunt belligerence that still, after six years, turned my stomach. The prisoners at the Walls rarely stole from each other; these kids made it the predominant tenet of their convoluted code of ethics. They called it "hogging," and much of their abundant energy went into its execution.

PACK II INMATES HOEING NEAR THE BRAZOS RIVER

Since coming to Pack II, a place full of kids who would have most of their lives left when they were released, I'd developed the beginnings of a credo about my work. I believed that the primary job of anyone working at a prison, from the guards to the warden, is to keep the inmates locked up, to keep the prison safe for all who live and work there, and to do so at a reasonable cost to the taxpayer. I didn't often see prisoners who seemed to want to straighten out their lives; inmates as trustworthy as Donald Walker were rare. But if a convict elected either to learn something or to turn over a new leaf, I believed that prison should offer training and encouragement to help him make it on the outside.

Right then, I wanted to believe that the Pack II inmates wanted nothing more than peaceful lives on the outside. I desperately wanted that lieutenant to call saying that the inmates had gone peacefully to their beds. I wanted another cold Pearl, too.

THE SECOND PHONE CALL CAME SIXTEEN MINUTES AFTER THE FIRST, AND THE lieutenant had crushed any hopes of a quiet night in the country. The inmates, he'd told me, had progressed from refusing to go to bed to throwing things at the guards. Some had lit small fires in the dorms. I told him to make sure his officers were safe and to get a riot team together, and that I'd be there soon. I called Warden Drewry and headed out. As I hurried across the footbridge that separated the duplex and the front gate, I could hear shouting inside the unit.

When I was nearly to the gate, a state-owned Dodge Ramcharger screeched to a halt beside me, and the senior warden got out. Ron Drewry was my fourth boss in six years, and I admired him. He was the six-foot, not-an-ounce-of-fat epitome of a long, tall Texan, and he dressed in western garb, complete with a black shirt, starched jeans, finely tooled boots, and a Stetson. He swaggered when he walked. Tonight, he swaggered briskly.

"Let's go see what we've got," he called.

Inside, the noise was nearly deafening. The young inmates were always loud, but I had never before heard a prison this noisy. The lieutenant had to shout to tell us what was already crystal-clear: that the correctional staff had lost control of the dorms. No one had been injured, he said, but several guards had been struck by thrown objects. We could hear more things being hurled against walls and bars.

Warden Drewry got quiet then, and thoughtful. Figuring out, I suspected, how best to employ the riot team that had already been assembled. I considered how I would use the team, in case he asked my opinion.

He didn't. He had a plan of his own.

THE PACK II UNIT, BUILT ON ADJOINING FERTILE, RIVER-BOTTOM FARMLAND WITH its neighbor, Pack I, was eight years old. The construction crews that built them used to stop at the Walls to load up on ice and drinking water, and we'd all wondered why the system was putting units out in the boondocks. Both the prison farms had been named for Wallace Pack, the warden Eroy Brown had drowned. Instead of cells, Pack II consisted of twenty dorms.

Crash gates were strategically placed to secure large areas, not unlike water-tight bulkheads in ships; there were crash gates between every set of four dorms. We stood outside the first crash gate and listened to the racket a moment before the warden announced his plan.

He didn't address the riot team. Instead, he put his hand on my shoulder. "Let's you and me go into every dorm," he said, "and see if we can't get 'em to get in their bunks."

I hoped I'd misunderstood him because of all the noise. Then I mustered all the confidence I could and said okay.

Drewry led the way, sweeping past the guard who opened the door to the first dorm. He shouted, "Get in those bunks!" A few seconds of stunned silence passed. He screamed, "Now!"

As I motioned for another guard to open the door to next dorm, I did some math. There were roughly a thousand inmates in this building and, this being a night shift and a holiday, fewer than forty officers — not the officer-to-inmate ratio one would hope for. I stepped in ahead of two officers, heard the door close behind us, and looked at fifty-four young men who looked back at me. At least three of them held things in midair, poised to throw.

I'd learned early that though juvenile inmates might formulate a goal, they rarely planned a way to accomplish it. I doubted that a riot had been even a goal;

CHAPTER THIRTEEN

AERIAL VIEW OF THE PACK II UNIT

this rowdiness looked spontaneous. But even so, my entrance with the men behind me made a bigger impression than I would have predicted.

I prayed they wouldn't call my bluff.

"Everybody on your bunks!" I said, loud, with as much force as I could muster. I tried to sound like the guy in charge.

Miraculously, they did what I said. They grumbled, took their time, and bitched. But they did it. I sent up another short prayer. This time, it was a thank-you note.

014

CRUMP LIKED ME BECAUSE I LIKED FLOWERS. IT WAS simple as that.

He was sixty-three years old and had spent most of those years in prison. Thin as a rail. Not very tall. White prison uniform a perfect fit on his lean, sturdy body, its color a sharp contrast against his black-as-midnight skin. He could outwork men half his age, and when he rested, he rested under the shade of trees that he had planted himself. He'd been at the Diagnostic Unit for an awfully long time.

He stood before me now in the tall rubber boots he wore when he was watering or working in the flower-beds. He was doing one or the other most of the time.

"This here's gonna be pertunias, I'm thinking." He pointed at a patch of freshly tilled loam and rubbed a big hand across his jaw. "And some impatiens" — he said "in-patients," as if it were a medical term — "over yonder." He pointed to another place. "There be more shade over yonder. Impatiens be needing shade, don't they?"

I nodded. Crump expended the energy and the muscle in this little operation of ours. But I had to help with seed varieties and the needs and traits of individual plants. His horticultural expertise didn't extend any further than knowing that things had to be carefully planted, lovingly tended, and sufficiently watered. That's all he needed to know. Because of him, the front of the Diagnostic Unit was a veritable

WILLIAM JEFFERSON CRUMP

park, with marigolds in summer and pansies all winter. There were daisies, kale, and all manner of shrubs and ground cover, even dwarf banana plants on the years that he felt they might thrive. The bananas weren't edible, but Crump didn't care. He just liked to hold them and look at them.

Because of his constant orchestration of sprinklers, the big lawn in front was always a lush, deep green.

He squinted in the bright sunshine and adjusted his cap until he had it just the way he wanted it. One of the convicts in the inmate laundry had made it for him, out of the same white material used for the uniforms. It had a shorter bill than most caps, and a taller front. Like a train conductor's cap.

"I'll be needin' some more mulch here directly," he told me, his voice as deep and rich as the topsoil he cultivated. "And fert-lizer. I need me a whole mess of fert-lizer."

We had other flowerbeds in other places, with other convicts in charge of them. But Crump didn't care anything about that. He wanted everything for his personal Garden of Eden. He'd shown annoyance a few times about what he considered my misallocation of materials. Crump argued that the real estate he tended was the first thing anyone saw of the prison, so it should be the most attractive. In point of fact, another inmate tended a large flowerbed by the highway, at our brick entrance. But that bed was not part of Crump's domain, so he simply disregarded its existence. William Jefferson Crump was not the sort of man to let mere facts dissuade him.

He worked constantly but slowly, as slowly as he talked and walked, but he could show anger on occasion. Perhaps that shouldn't have surprised me: He had been in and out of prison longer than I had been alive, and it's almost always anger that lands people there. His last sentence — the one that for all practical purposes insured that he would be locked up for the rest of his life — had been for cutting a woman who tried to steal two hundred dollars from him. That money had been issued to him a few hours earlier, when he'd been released from the penitentiary. The rest of his file logged a career in small-time crime: 1946, five years, robbery by assault; 1949, discharged; 1950, fifteen years, robbery by assault; 1959, discharged; short stretches throughout the sixties; a ten-year stint in the seventies and eighties for theft over $500, followed by a shorter one for theft under $200. Then that last one, with the woman who made the mistake of thinking that she could lift a little easy cash off an old man.

Now, in his seventh decade, about the most steam he could work up was about the new-fangled sprinklers I'd bought for him, telling me he'd spent enough time trying to figure them out and wanted the old kind. I went into town to purchase the right kind.

And then there had been the pear episode. He'd taken a pear from the dining hall to the trusty dorm. As a general rule, inmates weren't allowed to take food to their areas, but we made exceptions on special occasions such as Thanksgiving and Christmas. Crump apparently thought that the rare serving of pears constituted a special occasion. He'd intended to enjoy this one on his bunk,

CRUMP'S FLOWERS AND CREPE MYRTLES

slowly savoring every juicy morsel, but an officer had confiscated the forbidden fruit. When I arrived the next morning, Crump let me have an earful. Out of his sight, I called the kitchen and learned that all the pears were gone. That afternoon I stopped at a market in town and selected three nice Bartletts. I found Crump watering the front beds, gave him the pears, and told him not to take them in the unit.

He watched me now to make sure I had heard him about the fertilizer and the mulch. The sweat on his face sparkled in the midday sun. A thunderhead was building in the southwest, probably a summer shower working its way up from the Gulf. Crump studied the purplish line on the horizon, then looked at the sprinklers, calculating one of his many decisions of the day.

He decided to leave the sprinklers on awhile longer — he'd been fooled before by ominous-looking clouds that hadn't amounted to anything — and he got back to his digging.

"Them little trees be just about ready to bring out here in another day or two," he said, not looking up from his work. He'd dug up several crepe myrtle pups and had been nurturing them in the greenhouse for weeks.

"I know exactly where they going."

Which didn't come as any surprise to me. He undoubtedly knew down to the centimeter where he would locate them.

He'd come now to some rosebushes that he might have pruned back too far. He'd told me more than once that roses were moodier than he cared for. Aggravated, he walked to the pond to feed a group of ducks that I believe he considered his own. He always kept his pockets full of cornbread crumbs from the kitchen, and now he tossed a few crumbs to a couple of handsome black swans that one of my captains had provided. The old gander of the pair chased my secretary as often as he saw her. Crump threw extra crumbs to the gander. He admired spunk, even in a swan.

FOR ME, BEING TRANSFERRED TO DIAGNOSTIC FROM PACK II HAD MEANT COMING home. Home to my family, from whom I had been mostly separated for two years. Home to Huntsville, where I had spent most of my life. And home to a unit that was more like the Walls than the prison farm near Navasota. There was no field force, unless you counted Crump and his sprinklers, and the population was both very temporary and refreshingly older than the juvenile delinquents at Pack II. After six years, I'd had entirely enough of their antics.

Diagnostic was unique among Texas prisons in that the vast majority of its inmates weren't permanent residents. Except for a small group of prisoners assigned to work there, like Crump, most of the unit's inmates were fresh out of county jails, just starting their incarcerations. Those sentenced to be executed stayed only an hour before being transported to death row at the Ellis Unit. Most, though, stayed with us for two weeks, undergoing a barrage of interviews, medical examinations, and psychological and educational testing. They had their pictures taken and their criminal history dredged up. At the end, they were assigned to one of the many prisons throughout Texas, and were loaded on a white bus with other inmates, a driver, and an officer riding shotgun — literally riding shotgun, with a shotgun in his hands. On any given day, there were around 1300 inmates at Diagnostic, along with more than four hundred employees, including security officers, medical personnel, and classification staff.

The inmates assigned to the unit for the duration of their sentences were older than the Pack II boys, more dependable and easier to be around. Like Crump. And like Kenneth Stafford, the forty-something-year-old housekeeper in the duplex next to ours. He spent much of his time in a little room behind the garage that we shared with the neighbors, washing, ironing and folding clothes. A babysitter would bring our daughter Jordan home from elementary school every day, and Jordan would usually visit with Stafford for an hour or so until Janice and I got home. He was always kind to her, and we never felt nervous about her being in his company.

Some afternoons, Jordan would call to say she wanted to come to my office. She liked sitting in the outer office with my secretary, who often let her answer the switchboard. I never allowed her to do it until after four-thirty, when I figured nobody of any importance would call. One afternoon, I heard her say "Diagnostic Unit" in her sweet little-girl voice, then "Hold on, please." She called out that Wayne Scott was on the phone for me. I picked up and heard the amused voice of the director of the entire criminal justice system.

I hadn't been Warden Lanny Steele's first choice as his assistant, and he

TRUSTY KENNETH STAFFORD AND JORDAN WILLETT

hadn't made any bones about it. He'd wanted to promote his major at Diagnostic, a man who already knew the operation inside and out.

That's what he'd wanted. What he got was me.

I served a probationary period, though it was never labeled as such. He gave me an office back in the middle of the unit, rather than up front, close to his. I didn't even have an outside phone line, so every time I wanted to call somebody beyond our fences, I first had to call Steel's secretary to get a line. After about a year, I finally convinced Steele that I would do. I was brought up front, given a new office, and trusted with a phone that actually connected to the wide world.

When Lanny Steele decided to retire, I had a decision to make. I was a good assistant warden; I knew it, and so did the upper echelon of the system. I'd never been the sort who had to be in complete control, and in the periods between wardens at Pack II, I'd been in charge enough to know it was considerably easier to make suggestions than to make decisions. On the other hand, I knew I might end up working for someone who was, in my opinion, less qualified than I was. There were already several wardens throughout the system who had once worked under my supervision. I'd never perceived this as a slight, since I had never applied for a senior warden's slot, but the soul searching I did when Steele told me about his retirement ended with the decision that it was time for me to work for me. A senior warden was the head honcho of the unit. Period. Certainly there were people above him, higher-ups in the system, but the senior warden ran his prison. Like the captain of a warship at sea, he was the final authority in almost every situation.

I applied for the job, and in due course was assigned to be senior warden of the Diagnostic Unit. Janice, Jacob, Jordan and I packed everything in our house in the country and moved into the warden's residence on the unit. I couldn't have asked for a better place to serve as warden. Because of the nature of the work that we did, I had less paperwork than other wardens, which was fine with me. I had time to do what I liked best: move around the unit and visit each department every day. In my middle age, I had become a reincarnation of Walking George Beto. My staff was wonderful, the job was challenging and enjoyable, and the inmates assigned to us permanently were no problem.

Especially Crump.

He'd developed a fan club out there in front of the unit, in his conductor's cap and rubber boots. Most people who had regular business with us — wardens, assistant directors, and all manner of law-enforcement officials — usually stopped to visit with him, to tell him how nice he had the place looking. He'd smile. Sometimes he'd stop what he was doing and visit for a minute. Sometimes he tipped his cap. If he didn't like the looks of the visitor, he'd just nod and go on with whatever he was doing, as if no one was there at all.

HE PUSHED AT ONE OF THE ROSEBUSHES, BEING CAREFUL OF THE THORNS. I ASKED once if he wanted me to get him work gloves, but he said he didn't. Crump never asked for anything, other than things he needed for his plants and the lawn, and the day off every Valentine's Day, which was his birthday. He rarely had visitors; I think he had a sister somewhere, but she had obviously written him off long ago.

"Seems like," he said, "roses just got a mind of they own and like being ornery. Don't it?"

I'd had difficulties with roses myself, and told him it did sometimes seem like that.

He showed me one or two more things he wanted me to see, reminded me about the fertilizer and the mulch, and pointed at the dark sky off to the southwest. He said we might get us a little drink here directly, but he didn't much think so. I went in to work.

Several hours later, when the thunderhead had rumbled its farewell and moved off to the north without spilling so much of a drop of rain, the officer in the number one picket called me to report that she had been watching Crump all afternoon. She told me that he had gone, three times, down under a bridge on the highway that runs beside the unit.

"He's out of my sight down there, Warden," she told me.

We were both quiet for a moment.

"I can't see him," she said. In case I had missed the point.

"He's probably going down there to relieve himself," I suggested. "He's an old man. I imagine he has to do that pretty often."

"I thought of that," she said. "But if he's going down there that often to take a leak, then he's got one major bladder problem."

We were quiet again. I was fully aware of what was going on. Crump had smoked a couple of packs of cigarettes every day since his childhood — that is,

AERIAL VIEW OF THE DIAGNOSTIC UNIT

until a year ago, when we banned tobacco throughout the system. He hadn't been alone in the agony that came with quitting cold turkey; almost all of our convicts had depended heavily on nicotine. I had no doubt that the old man had somehow come by a pack of smokes. Down under that bridge, he was giving his old lungs a trip down memory lane.

"He's just gone down there again," the officer told me, with enough of an edge in her voice to convince me that I would have to take some sort of action.

So I did.

I told her I'd take care of it. She was a fine officer and would work well anywhere in the unit. So I got her lieutenant on the phone and told him to make sure that, after today, she would be assigned somewhere other than the number one picket.

EXECUTION JOURNAL

Number fourteen
November 17, 1998

Kenneth McDuff is in a lousy mood, Chaplain Brazzil tells me the morning of McDuff's execution date. But I find it difficult to work up much interest in the disposition of death row inmate no. 999055, a murderer who slaughtered so many people that officials are still digging up their bodies.

Apparently McDuff had been convinced that the courts would intervene at the last moment. But now that the day has arrived, and the last moment is only eight hours away, he has begun to face reality. The chaplain visited death row at Ellis this morning, and he reports that McDuff is lying on his bunk, curled in the fetal position, with only the very top of his head emerging from a blanket. He is talking to no one.

After lunch, McDuff's mother and some of his nieces and nephews show up at Ellis too late to visit him; a white prison van is already carrying him to the Walls. When he arrives, I go back to the cellblock in the death house to talk to him. Internal Affairs people are already there, trying to wring additional information from him regarding other possible victims. His doldrums seem to have passed.

His file told me he is fifty-two years old, three inches over six feet tall, and weighs a little over two hundred and fifty pounds. It didn't tell me that his gaze is wolf-like. Or that his narrow eyes dart constantly.

He clenches the bars with his big hands. Looks at me with his wolf eyes.

"I understand you're the man to see about some cigarettes," he says, loud enough for people outside in the upper yard to hear him. The other people in the block stop what they're doing and watch us.

I've broken a well-established rule in this room many times, and Chaplain Brazzil has been my accessory. The way I figure it, it can't do any harm to provide a couple of smokes to somebody about to die. Sometimes the chaplain would mention this to death row inmates a day or so before they were brought to the Walls, and would even teach them the codeword that we had devised. Sometimes, when I'd talk to a convict on the afternoon before his execution, he'd forget the magic word. Brazzil would say something like "Didn't you want to ask the warden about Joe?"

I never let them light up until after I'd left, but I could imagine them sucking the smoke down as deep as they could get it, holding it there as long as they could, then blowing it out slowly. In many cases, I suspect it was more satisfying than the last meal.

We probably never fooled any of my staff with our codified shenanigans, but I trust my people, and if anyone has a problem with the procedure, they would already have told me. But not all the people in here now are my staff.

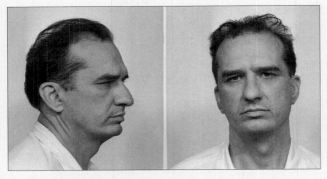

KENNETH MCDUFF, DEATH ROW INMATE NO. 999055

And we aren't likely to fool anybody after McDuff's outburst. I ask how long it's been since he's had one.

His eyes go narrower. He's considering something. Maybe his answer. Maybe whether he'll provide an answer.

"Right before they put me on the death watch." Now his voice is more like an animal's growl than any sound a human might make. It is coarse, almost guttural, as if it hasn't been used regularly in a long time. He looks down at me, and points down the block to the stack of the bags containing his personal property. "Those two that are wrapped up are clocks," he says. "I built them myself."

He makes a come-here motion, as if he expects the bags to come on their own. "I want to show you something."

An assistant warden and a sergeant from the Ellis Unit start unwrapping the parcels. The sergeant finishes his first. He brings the wooden clock case over to the bars. McDuff smiles, reaches inside, and fishes out a small plastic bag holding a cigarette lighter.

I don't stay long enough to see, but I'd bet good money that the other clock contains cigarettes.

███

The media descend on us all afternoon. Satellite dishes and antennas sprout out the tops of TV and radio vans; thick cables spill out their sides. A big crowd gathers. McDuff was front-page material when he was killing, and again when he was captured. Now he's in the limelight one last time.

In 1965 he was sentenced to his first stretch — four years — for burglary in Bell, Milam, and Falls counties, and was paroled within a year. The next October, he killed two teenaged boys and raped and strangled their female companion. He received the death penalty for those crimes, but his timing was good. Before his scheduled execution, the Supreme Court ruled the procedure unconstitutional, and the governor of Texas commuted all fifty-two cases on death row to life. McDuff was paroled in 1989. Three years later, after the disappearance of at least nine women, he was the subject of a nationwide manhunt. He was arrested in Kansas City, Missouri, then tried and convicted to die, specifically for the murder of a twenty-two-year-old Waco woman.

Mid-afternoon his mother calls and tells me how she'd missed having a last visit with him this morning. She asks to be allowed to see him now. I tell her I can't do that. She cries and says she can't understand why. I tell her that it just can't happen. A few minutes later, one of the nephews calls — maybe the one who caused them to be late getting to the Ellis Unit — and wants the same thing. I give the same answer. When they arrive at the Walls, Chaplain Brazzil visits with them and comes back into my office to tell me they're upset. About this time McDuff is having his last meal in his cell. He asked for two sixteen-ounce T-bone steaks, five fried eggs, French fries, vegetables, coconut pie, and a Coca-Cola. Instead of the steaks, he's been given broiled hamburger patties, since the prison system hasn't provided steaks — to anyone, condemned or not — for a long while.

A few minutes before six I call the attorney general's office in Austin to find out where we are. Still in the Supreme Court, they tell me. This is beginning to have all the markings of a long night. And everybody — I mean everybody — is here, standing in small groups in my office and the one just outside it. The director is talking to the executive director and the regional director. Even the chairman of the State Board of Criminal Justice has driven up for this one. It wouldn't surprise me to look up and see Governor Bush come in.

Less than ten minutes later my contact in the attorney general's office calls to tell me the Supreme Court has denied the request for a stay. So we all return to the death house to wait for the two official calls: one from the attorney general again, the other from the governor's office. Both say to proceed.

I step into the row, go to McDuff's cell, and tell him it's time. An officer unlocks the two Master locks on the heavy chain looped through the door and the bars, then the lock on the cell door itself. Though McDuff had said earlier he'd have to be dragged, kicking and screaming, he falls in behind me, walks down the block and into the execution chamber, and lies down on the gurney.

KENNETH MCDUFF ARRIVES AT THE DEATH HOUSE. (CHAPLAIN BRAZZIL IN THE FOREGROUND.)

The medical team does its work quickly. The witnesses — Major Katherine Cox of the Salvation Army, two of McDuff's nieces, two of his nephews, and six members of his victims' families — are brought in to the gallery. They listen to McDuff's one-sentence last statement: "I am ready to be released."

In not too many minutes, he is. I send him to the Huntsville Funeral Home. Tomorrow we'll bury him at Joe Byrd Cemetery.

By the time I walk out of the Walls, most of the media and the crowd have gone home. The protestors are gone too, except for the one group that stands a candlelight vigil every time we do this. They're grouped together down the street, their small flames blinking in the darkness.

Executions are still the worst part of my job. Hands down. On many of these nights I feel emotionally connected to the execution, even when I try hard not to. Almost always I've sympathized with the inmate's family on the other side of the window, watching their son or husband or father. Watching me. Watching for my signal. And there have even been nights when my heart — at least part of it — has gone out to the inmate himself, stretched out on the gurney.

Not tonight.

Tonight, no matter what the opponents of capitol punishment might say, I know that we've ridded the world of a man that it will be better off without. Tonight, for once, the flickering candles inspire no doubt.

015

BIRDS WERE SINGING. THE SUN WAS SHINING. IT WAS A nice spring morning, a Tuesday, with the East Texas winter behind us and the long, blistering summer still to come. A few cars and pickups headed down the hill toward the courthouse square. Huntsville was up and running, and I had the shortest commute in town: less than a hundred yards from the senior warden's residence to the front porch of the Walls. The guard in the number one picket called out good morning as I walked beside flowers that old Crump would have been proud of.

The plants along the sidewalk were starting to bloom: petunias, marigolds, and verbena. The winter pansies had just about played out; I made a mental note to tell the trusty who tended the beds to dig them out and replace them with something more tolerant of summer heat.

The big clock read seven-thirty. Inside at the sign-in window, I showed my ID card to the radio picket officer, who pushed a button on her intercom to signal the guard in the swinging picket to roll the door. A steady whirring commenced, and the heavy steel bars slid slowly away. I stepped into my day.

Framed photographs of the unit, taken over the last century and a half, covered one side of the wide hallway opposite my office. At the end of the hall the shining bars of the bull ring formed the boundary of

THE BRASS BARS AND SHINING FLOORS OF THE BULL RING

the prison proper. Past those bars, beyond the administrative offices and visitation area, nobody ever had the slightest doubt as to where they were. When those weighty brass beauties clanged shut behind you, you knew full well that you were indeed incarcerated, surrounded completely in a huge cage that we used mostly as a holding pen for convicts who had business up front — usually a visit with a family member or, less happily, with me.

A secretary said hello, and the inmate porter assigned to the office nodded as I entered. He'd already started the coffee in a big urn that was gasping out the message that it was near the end of its process. And he'd filled a five-gallon stainless steel container with ice and water, and hung a metal ladle on its handle. Beads of sweat as large as pebbles glistened on the cold surface. There would be hot coffee all morning for staff and visitors, and iced water all day long. He poured me a cup of the coffee and followed me into my office, where he helped me out of my jacket and hung it up. Then he went back out into the other room to wait for the clerks and secretaries to arrive.

Other rooms I'd been assigned in my career had been tiny compared to this one, built in a different century. If the computer and telephone were erased from the picture, this one would probably look exactly as it had in the early 1900s. A wide desk in the center. One massive window that reached the high ceiling. Walls covered with thick panels of wood, old and rich and dark.

A tall bookcase was crammed full of manuals from the Texas Department of Criminal Justice. There was a particularly uncomfortable sofa, two armchairs, and a couple of tables. One was covered with magazines and some back issues of the Echo, the inmate-produced system-wide newspaper which was written and printed down in the lower yard. Framed photographs of Jacob and Jordan hung over the credenza behind the desk; other frames on other walls held an aerial shot of the sprawling unit and a floor plan of the place, dated 1930.

I settled into the high-backed chair at the desk, checked my e-mail, sipped the strong joe, and started work on things that I hadn't finished the day before. If tomorrow turned out like most days, I'd likely start it doing things I wouldn't finish today.

The next time I looked up, Tim New was lowering himself into one of the chairs in front of the desk as the porter put a cup of coffee on the side table. I told my assistant warden good morning, and the porter went out.

"There's a tour coming in at two," he said, looking at the planner he held open in his lap. "From a community college. Don't remember from where. I'll check. I'd take it all myself, but the teacher specifically asked for you for back there." He pointed in the direction of back there.

We were both quiet a moment while I finished tapping out an e-mail. Then I looked at him over the half-rims that I now needed to read anything at all.

"What sort of a class is it?"

"Criminology," Tim said.

I nodded. "I guess we know what they're coming to see."

Tim looked at his planner again. Flipped one page over.

"That won't be a problem. We don't have anything on in there till next week."

We talked about other things — the majority of things we did had nothing to do with what happened back there — and Tim returned to his own office. I took off my glasses, leaned back in my chair, and finished my coffee.

For good or ill, I was back where I'd started. The front steps I'd first climbed almost three decades ago lay a lazy stone's toss away; a heftier throw would reach the number one picket, where I'd nervously spent my first night on duty. Being called back to the Walls had been at once a homecoming and a dilemma. It had meant a substantial raise in pay, the opportunity to be in charge of what most people considered the flagship of the system, and ending up where I'd started, which somehow seemed the right way to go about things. The dilemma grew out of the business back there.

I'd talked the job over with Janice, who listened carefully as I rattled off positives and negatives before suggesting that I pray about it. As usual, I followed her advice. The next morning, I'd gone to see Lepher Jenkins, who told me I was at the top of the list for the post. I told him how honored I was to have been considered but that, strictly because of the executions, I'd decided to decline. He was disappointed, and I told him that, if they worked their way through the short list and still wanted me, I might reconsider. They had. And I did.

When I looked up this time, Chaplain Brazzil was leaning through the door, tapping his wristwatch. "Two this morning, Warden," he said, stepping over to hand me a couple of sheets of paper.

I put my glasses back on: One from Darrington and one from Retrieve. I pushed the papers away. "Expecting any family?"

"The brother of the one from Darrington is bringing their mother."

Back into my jacket. We headed for my car, a light blue Crown Victoria that came with the job, and commenced the short journey. In less than five minutes we pulled over beside Captain Joe Byrd Cemetery, named after an assistant warden at the Walls who spruced the place up and replaced the markers on inmates' graves. But that official name had never stuck. To prison and Huntsville folk, the place has been Peckerwood Hill since before the Civil War, when the first dead convict was planted there.

The cemetery occupied a wide, rolling hillside at the edge of town. The green grass was well tended, the pines towering, the white markers in long rows. When Captain Byrd started his restoration, he'd found the place in a hell of a mess. The oldest graves had been marked with wooden crosses; either no Jews were ever carried up the hill or, most likely, they were buried as Christians. Most of those crosses were either rotted beyond recognition or gone completely. Byrd had replaced them with simple white concrete crosses, handmade by inmates. Around the turn of the century, after the great Galveston hurricane swept over the hillside, uprooting many of the wooden crosses, the decision had been made to start using concrete tablets; later came concrete crosses bearing only the inmates' prison number and the date of death. Now we were back to tablets again, curved at the top, but with the inmate's name over his number and death date. An X in front of the number marked those who had been executed.

About a dozen trusties were charged with digging the graves, keeping the place mowed and tended, and making the concrete markers. The men came down the hill with the officer in charge of them. You could tell by looking that they worked outside: They wore baseball caps, and their bodies showed muscle. Clay was never easy to dig; it was either too wet or too dry. And we didn't have a backhoe, only shovels. Prisons didn't need labor-saving devices; labor was our most abundant resource.

We watched the Huntsville Funeral Home van come slowly over the top of the hill and make its way down the street. It stopped behind my car, and an old Buick pulled up behind it. There wasn't any other traffic on the street, no walkers

CAPTAIN JOE BYRD CEMETERY

or joggers or bicyclists, nothing else going on at all.

The man from the funeral home opened the doors on the back of the van. He indicated which of the two pine caskets the trusties should slide out. As they carried it to one of the freshly dug graves, the old car's doors opened, and a family in church clothes slowly appeared. A black man, in his late sixties I'd guess, and a woman of about the same age. They helped a much older woman from the back seat. The paperwork the chaplain had handed me in my office had said the convict was sixty-seven. The old woman, almost certainly in her nineties, was the right age to be his mother.

The inmate had spent most of his life in Texas prisons, and had died of natural causes at the Darrington Unit in Brazoria County. I thought of Crump for the second time this morning as I glanced up the hill toward his grave. More than a few prison officials had come to Crump's funeral; I'd never seen that happen, and I'd attended quite a few services on the gentle slope of this hill. It was one of the duties unique to me, since all deceased inmates in the entire system whose bodies were not claimed by their families were buried here by a detail from the Walls.

The chaplain introduced us to the family, and we followed the procession to the graves. The trusties placed the casket on the metal platform that straddled the grave, then they moved back, with their officer, to a shady spot. The rest of us gathered around the casket. The two younger family members held tight to the old woman, who was thin and frail and unsteady on her feet. She wore a wide-brimmed hat that matched her dress, and she clutched a handkerchief in a hand that looked too small and brittle to lift even that.

The chaplain said a prayer, read a scripture, and said a few words. Then he asked if the family would like to say anything.

The man looked at the grave for a moment, then at the old woman.

"Will it be all right," he said, looking first at the chaplain and then at me, "if my mother sings a little?"

Brazzil said that would be fine.

The old woman listened and wobbled a bit as the man whispered something to her. She took a short step forward, and we all waited as she made sure of her balance. Then she closed her eyes and sang the first stanza of "Amazing Grace" in a trembling, low voice. She paused after the first verse, long enough that I thought she was done. But after a moment, she launched into the second stanza.

She found more vigor, and the words were clearer. By the time she had worked her way through to the last verse — "when we've been there ten thousand years" — the words rose clear and strong through the tall pines and the bright morning.

When they were gone, the trusties came back down the hill and moved the other casket to the other grave. Since no family had shown up for this man, the inmates and their officer came close while the chaplain performed the ritual. Then the man from the funeral home drove away, the chaplain and I went back to the car, and the trusties took up their shovels and went to work.

By the end of the year, if it was like most other years, they'd have buried around a hundred inmates at Peckerwood Hill, old men and a few old women who ended their days in a prison.

On the way back to the Walls, the chaplain folded the papers that represented the two convicts and slipped them into the inside pocket of his suit coat.

"She had a pretty voice, didn't she?" he said. "The old woman."

I nodded, and watched the red brick walls come into view.

016

I POKED MY HEAD INTO THE CLASSIFICATION COMMITTEE room — in the basement of the chapel, beside the count room — to let Tim New see that I was back on the unit. The committee met every morning starting at nine, and the assistant warden sat in for me on days that I had to attend burials. Or when I could find any reason to be anywhere else.

All inmates who had to be classified or reclassified had to go before this group, made up of the senior or the assistant warden and one representative each from the security, medical, and treatment staffs. When prisoners first arrived at the Walls, this committee assigned them to specific jobs. If someone already in the Walls population got into trouble, the disciplinary captain decided how much of his good behavior time got yanked, but this committee decided whether he would be shipped to another unit. The meeting sometimes ran to eleven or later, and the warden who started it always finished it. So on the days that Tim chaired it, I could catch up on other things.

In my outer office, Bobbie waved a stack of papers at me and said she needed five minutes. Kim reminded me that I had a group coming for a tour at two. Shanda said the fire and safety man was on his way up from the lower yard and needed a few minutes. I thanked God that Terry was on the phone, so she couldn't add something to the mix.

JIM AND THE SECRETARIES WHO WORKED FOR HIM FROM 1993 TO 2001.
LEFT TO RIGHT: LINDA LAMPSON, SHANDA PEGODA, RITA HEATON, JIM WILLETT,
MOLLY STANDLEY, JANNA GRIGGS, CONNIE ADAMS, AND KIM HUFF.

The porter followed me into my office, helped me out of my coat, hung it up, and asked if I wanted coffee. He knew I never did, this late in the morning, but he always asked. He went out and came back in with a glass of iced water instead. He had precious few duties, this old convict, and his primary goal was to hang on to this air-conditioned plum of an assignment. So he kept the trashcans empty, the floor clean, and beverages at hand.

Nine while-you-were-out phone messages were laid out on my desk like a single row of solitaire. By the time I sat down and was staring at them, the fire and safety man was standing in the open door. He was in charge of making sure that nothing violated codes, not an easy task in this huge prison, some of whose buildings had already been old when his great-great-grandfather had been his age.

"Warden," he said, "in the craft shop I found some canisters of chemicals that we have to do something about." He fired off names that meant nothing to me and dropped his report on the small mountain of papers on my desk. "We'll need to buy a cabinet to store them in. Maintenance won't be able to build one 'cause it'll have to meet spec. Lots of vents. Fireproofed. We're in violation of code. Big time."

He told me more things. I nodded. Jotted a couple of them down. Watched him leave.

I lifted the first of the message slips and punched in the numbers for my regional director, who wanted to know whether the nine o'clock count had cleared. It had. The next voice in my receiver belonged to Larry Fitzgerald, the public information director, who told me about two reporters — one from a paper in Chicago, the other from somewhere in Europe — who had requested interviews, both about executions. They were always about executions; nobody ever wanted to talk about rehabilitation, or education, or the public service projects that some of our convicts did. Our inmates made toys for orphans, raised money for a child burn victim, and bought canned food at the commissary to donate to the poor. That wasn't news. Me taking off my glasses and shutting a human life down was news. Larry gave me the names and the dates, and I penciled them into my planner.

Next up was a woman in San Antonio whose son's radio had been confiscated by an officer.

"I sent him twenty dollars for it," she bellowed into the phone. "And I ain't got twenty dollars to throw away, I can tell you."

I held the receiver further from my ear and asked her to repeat her son's name so I could write it down. She did — slowly and loudly — then cut to the chase.

"I want to know why they took up my boy's radio. He says there ain't no rule there about having a radio. I want to know when he's gonna get it back."

I told her I'd check with the officer who confiscated it, and somebody would get back to her.

"I paid twenty dollars for it," she told me again before I managed to ring off. Inmates were allowed to have headphones only. I suspected that the kid had somehow hooked a stereo speaker to the radio. And when the guard heard music playing in the cellblock, he'd confiscated the whole rig and turned it in to the property officer. If that was the case, the kid would have to say goodbye to the radio, and his mother would be out her twenty bucks.

I looked at the remaining message slips, at a stack of requests from inmates, and then at the clock. The San Antonio woman's piercing voice still rang in my ears, and I made an executive decision that a short break from the telephone was in order. In the outer office, I told the secretaries that I was stepping across the hall for a haircut and a shoeshine.

Three convicts were "laid in," sitting on a bench in the bull ring, waiting for interviews. Two officers at the searchers' desk nodded at me; the old barber met me at the door of his shop. I settled into a chair that had seen most, and maybe all, of the century that we had just finished. The barber snapped the apron shut, then took a comb in one hand and a pair of shears in the other.

"Nice morning, Warden," he said, snipping away. His scissors wisped along; little specks of gray hair fell away; and on the TV, Bob Barker summoned contestants from The Price Is Right audience.

"Be awful nice to be fishing on a morning like this one," the barber said. He'd been in since 1982, convicted of killing his wife, a crime he never denied. He was a good barber, but he was feeling his age. Men age faster in prison than in the free world, and barbers' legs and feet age faster than the rest of their bodies. He had a hard time standing up all day. Eventually he'd have to be reassigned to the night brass squad, where he could sit on a stool and polish the brass bars in the bull ring — the job of old convicts who couldn't do anything else.

Being assigned to polish brass bars was the prison's equivalent of setting an old Eskimo adrift on an ice floe. It was the end of the line. We already had a couple of former barbers on the night squad, along with some former shop and laundry workers. Crump wouldn't have made a good polisher, or at least a happy one; he'd have hated sitting all the time in a place without sunshine or flowers.

But Crump had been in excellent physical condition till the end, which was hardly ever the case for old convicts. This barber was obviously nearing the end of the line, and just as obviously, he was trying to hang on as long as he could.

Inmate jobs are a good deal for the prison system. Prisoner labor saves the taxpayers money. At the Walls, where the population was older than average, we often received inmates who already had good work habits and useful skills. With no further training, a man who'd been an auto mechanic in the free world could start work in the prison system's main auto shop — and immediately he'd earn his keep. Even better, from the prison system's point of view, the jobs prevented idleness. A busy inmate was less likely to make trouble.

But the jobs were good for the men who did them, too. Time passes awfully slowly when you have no purpose; even making license plates is better than sitting in your cell all day, doing nothing. But many inmates try to make something of themselves, to learn a trade while in prison. Some take vocational classes, and some learn by doing; a man with no previous experience might find himself in the mechanical department, and would learn the trade there. Either way, the inmate would feel progress, a sense that he'd be better when he got out than when he went in.

But for men like Crump and the barber, their jobs went deeper. Their jobs weren't just something to do, and they already knew everything there was to know about their little worlds. What they did was who they were: Crump was a gardener; this man was a barber. He was good at cutting hair, and he liked the talk that went with it. Polishing brass wasn't a terrible job, but it wasn't barbering. When he could no longer be a barber, a piece of him would die.

He talked about fishing some more, and told me again that he'd be up before the parole hearing soon. When he finished the haircut, he brushed talcum powder on my neck and swept my hair from the floor.

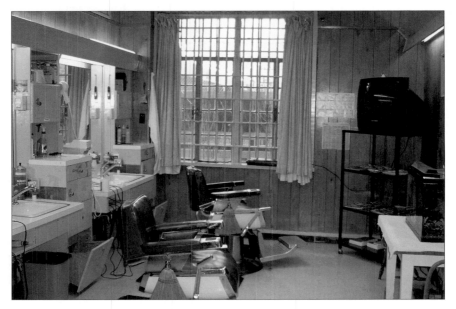

BARBER SHOP AT THE WALLS

I got a shoeshine from another inmate, and was back at my desk by 10:30. I returned calls, including two that had come while I was at the barbershop, then dug into the stack of I-60s. The official name of the form was "Request to Official"; we never used that name. Every day brought a new stack of I-60s, and each of them represented somebody who wanted something.

I dealt with the easy ones first, the clear-cut yeses or nos. Then I called out to Bobbie to pull the files on a couple of others, the ones about which I'd need to talk to the major, or maybe even the inmate himself. Then there were always two or three requests to see me in person; I looked these over and scribbled a note on them so that one of the secretaries could lay in those inmates for interviews with me that afternoon.

A sergeant came to the door and waited till I looked up to speak.

"Warden, there's a man outside asking to talk to you." He read the question in my eyes. "I've been visiting with him out front. He and his wife have been out there a couple of hours now. He really would like to see you just a minute."

The man was waiting on the front porch, leaning against the brass rails. When he saw me, he stood up as straight as he could. An old pair of khaki pants and a faded cotton shirt covered a slight body that had obviously been worked hard for a long time.

"I thank you for coming out to talk to me," he started. I could tell he was speaking more quickly than he was used to, not wanting to take up any more of my time than necessary. "Our boy called us yesterday and told us we was to pick him up right here this morning." He pointed a leathery, sun-baked hand down at the porch, then at a tall woman sitting at one of the picnic tables in the plaza across the street. She wasn't watching us, but gazed down at her hands that were folded in her lap.

"And now they tell me he won't be getting out today at all." He pronounced it *a-tall*, with no more emphasis on it than he had placed on any of the other words. He pointed to the door behind me, I suppose in the direction of the clerk that had given him the news.

"We come all the way from just the other side of Amarillo." Now he looked at the woman again. Amarillo was about five hundred miles from Huntsville.

"We had to stop pretty often," he told me. "To put water into the radiator of our truck."

PICNIC TABLE IN PLAZA ACROSS STREET FROM THE WALLS

I looked over at the visitor's parking lot, and located what I would have bet a paycheck was the vehicle they'd come in. It was a Chevy, badly in need of paint, old enough to have wheel wells that protruded away from the body, and running boards.

"We ain't got enough money to put up in any motel," he said. "We aimed to head right on back today."

He wasn't angry when he said it. He held his cap in his hands, and he looked worn out. From hard life, and a hard drive that was only half over. And no doubt from this bad business of his son.

It was a common scenario. Almost every inmate released from a Texas prison took his first step into freedom out the Walls' front door. About of third of them were lucky enough to have someone who cared enough to pick them up. The picnic tables and benches outside were usually occupied by families there to collect sons or brothers or friends or fathers who had done their time. Many times, the county where the crime had been committed would protest the release, then all the legal technicalities would place the whole process on ice for a few weeks. The sergeant had told me, as we'd come out of my office, that this was the case with this man's son.

I walked across the street with him, and he introduced me to his wife, who stood up to meet me. She was as exhausted as he was. She watched me while I told them there was nothing I could do, and that her son wouldn't be released anytime soon. Then she looked at the red-bricked fortress in front of her. At the big clock overhead.

"Can we at least talk to him?" she asked. "Before we leave?"

I thought about her request. Visiting days were Saturdays and Sundays, and the official line was that there were no exceptions. But the official line didn't take into account how much it means for a former inmate to have someone on the outside who'll help him stay out of prison. This couple didn't have money, but the support they'd give their son was worth more. I didn't have statistics, but common sense told me that an inmate who was picked up was less likely to return to prison than an inmate who caught the bus.

I told the couple to follow me. Inside, I told the sergeant to have the inmate brought up from the transient block to the bull ring, then showed the man and his wife where they would need to stand and wait.

"You'll have to talk to him through the bars," I said. "And just for a few minutes."

The man thanked me, and shook my hand. His wife listened as I told them I was sorry. Then she said what she had obviously been thinking.

"I just don't understand why we can't take my boy home," she said. "If he's paroled." She said paroled as if it were magical, something only a wizard could bring about.

I talked a minute or two about district attorneys and judges and bench warrants. But she wasn't listening. She was already seeing the empty place on the pickup seat where she wanted her son to be. She was already focused on that thousand miles they would have driven at the end of all this, if the old truck made it back to the Texas Panhandle. And the thousand more that they'd have to drive in a couple of weeks, when the boy would finally be released. I almost reminded them of the bus station down the hill, and of the ticket home their son would be provided. But I didn't.

Since I'd been appointed senior warden, I'd looked many times out my office window at people like this sitting at the tables in the plaza. Many of them appeared

PREVIOUS PAGES: AERIAL VIEW OF THE WALLS

to be good, decent folks who life had just dealt a bad hand, and who had served every minute of a judge's sentence outside the prison, waiting for their sons to return. I blame a lot of crime on bad parenting, but I didn't blame the parents waiting at the tables. Television, maybe, or a bad crowd — something else had gotten hold of their boy.

Back inside, I took more calls and read reports. I took off my glasses, rubbed eyes that had read too much already, and told the ladies I was going to get a bite. The officer in the swinging picket rolled the doors, and I walked past the bull ring. The little couple from West Texas stood at the bars, talking to their son. The three nodded and whispered, and didn't appear to be surprised by the setback. The inmate had been in long enough to expect things not to go his way, and his parents looked like they'd lived a long time on the other side of the highway from good fortune. They had learned to take whatever happened as the way things had to be.

Past the searcher's desk, I stepped into a day that had grown into a beauty, then into the officer's dining room, still where it had always been, directly under the education department Carrasco and his accomplices had seized a quarter century before. I slid one of the big plastic trays along the rails and served myself meatloaf, green beans, a tossed salad, and a hot roll. An inmate waiter asked what I'd like to drink. He was new to the job. Soon, like all the others, he'd bring a glass of iced tea every time without asking. The prison system provided all employees with two meals a day, which meant that I had eaten well over fifteen thousand prison meals, the vast majority of them in this room. The food was always good.

I sat down at a table of officers. The conversation stopped just long enough for them to tell me hello.

"Hope the Astros are worth a damn this year."

"Dierker's a good manager."

"Takes more than a good manager. Takes pitching."

"Takes hitting, too."

"We got hitting. What we need is pitching."

"What I need is to quit hearing about the damn Astros all the time. What I need is a couple of days up at the deer lease. To put some corn in my feeders. To get away from the old lady."

They were quiet for a moment, while the inmate waiter asked me if I wanted him to bring dewberry cobbler and ice cream. I did.

"Biggio and Bagwell. That's the hitting. We need pitching."

I only half listened now, and let the afternoon stretch out before me. Those students from the community college were probably eating their lunch down the hill at McDonald's or the Golden Corral. Wondering what it would be like in here. Wondering what it would be like back there.

The little family was gone when I walked past the bull ring — the parents on the long road back to Amarillo, the boy back in his cell in the transient block. This morning the sergeant had told me the boy had served his stretch at the Beto unit. His stay with us would end tomorrow, and he'd ride a chain bus back there to stay another couple of weeks. If things didn't go well for him, he'd be there longer.

Back at my desk, I checked my e-mail, tapped out replies, and signed papers Kim brought in to me. Diane, the human resources supervisor, stepped in the door to remind me I had an employee disciplinary hearing and handed me a file.

"He's out here now, Warden," she said. I nodded that she should send him in.

Then the officer stood nervously in front of my desk. I rose and shook his hand as Diane pulled the door shut. When we all were seated, I picked up the folder.

"I haven't read this yet," I told the officer. "I'll read it right now, out loud, and then you can tell me your side of the story.

"Yes, sir," he said.

I put on my half frames and started. The charging officer, a sergeant, alleged that this young fellow had gone sound asleep in his picket — number five, on the southeast corner over the lower yard. The sergeant had not only seen the guard sleeping, he'd heard him snoring.

I closed the report, leaned back in the chair, and took off my glasses. The kid grimaced; maybe he'd heard that I removed my glasses to signal the executioner.

"Is that what happened?" I asked.

"Yes, sir." He looked down at the floor for a few seconds, then back at me. "I'd been out partying the night before and stayed up too late and drank too much. Up in the picket, I started nodding off. I guess I dropped off that one time, and went to sleep for a few minutes."

I watched him. And I remembered another kid in a picket who had made too much of a night of it at the Risin' Sun and had trouble keeping his eyes open. That fellow, with Willett on the nametag, had wandered in to work feeling like hell on a few occasions.

"Going to sleep with a loaded shotgun isn't the best of ideas in any situation," I told him. "And certainly not when you've got an important job to do."

I looked down at the report again. If there had been any discrepancy, or if he had denied the allegation, I would have tabled the matter, and called the sergeant in and questioned him. But now all I had to do was mete out the punishment.

The paperwork told me this was his first infraction. I'd long been of the opinion that the most lenient retribution worked best for first-time offenders, either inmates or officers. If an employee was a bad egg, he or she would end up back in front of me; there would be plenty more times to act more harshly. Of course, if the first-timer's charge was sufficiently serious — such as theft, or having sex with an inmate — then the first time would be the only time. But for falling asleep on duty, the fat manuals on my bookshelves gave me a range of options. I chose the least severe.

"You're on probation for six months, starting today," I said. "That means you can't be promoted, either automatically or to a slot you might want to go up for."

He said he understood. We both signed the report, stood up, shook hands.

"You have the right to file a grievance about my decision," I told him. "And if you do, and the punishment is overturned, I won't hold it against you."

He nodded. "I won't be filing one," he said. He straightened his belt, then tucked his gray uniform shirt in a little better.

"This won't happen again, sir," he said. "You can count on that."

I told him it would be best if it didn't, then he and Diane thanked me and left.

I sank back into the big office chair, swiveled around, and looked out my big window at a beautiful spring afternoon. On such a gem of a day, after such a good lunch, it seemed a shame that a man couldn't just stretch out for a half hour and concentrate on nothing more than the backs of his eyelids.

But as the afternoon bore heavily down, a bus bearing the name of a community college hissed to a stop outside the window. I leaned back up in my chair, and any notion of relaxing for a few minutes disappeared as quickly as the radio the San Antonio woman had paid her hard-earned money for.

017

TIM NEW CAME IN AND TOLD ME THE COLLEGE CLASS had arrived for their tour. Which was hardly news to me, since I had watched through the window as they climbed off their bus.

"They're upstairs in the turn-out room," he said. The porter stood beside him, holding my jacket spread-eagled for me to slip into.

Twenty-three students, none more than a couple of years out of high school, sat in the uncomfortable chairs where several times a day, officers waited to hear their duty assignments. The turn-out room was the closest thing we had to an auditorium.

The kids turned to watch Tim and me come in. Their professor stepped up quickly and pumped our hands, reminding us that he came every semester. I recognized him. He always told me, usually more than once, that he opposed the death penalty. He assumed, of course, that I was all for it. Most people believed I had to be, to do what I did.

But this fellow would be as wrong in labeling me a proponent of capital punishment as anyone who pegged me as the opposite. I pitched my tent in the vast middle ground. When I read in the paper that a twelve-year-old girl had been abducted, raped, and killed, I thought that the killer deserved to die, and that the state had every reason to demand that. But I had my doubts that the death penalty was fairly

JIM WILLETT ADDRESSES A HIGH SCHOOL CLASS. TIM NEW SITS BEHIND HIM ON A TABLE.

distributed among the rich and the poor, and possibly among the races. I didn't think it was efficient; even the guiltiest can tie up the courts for years. And I thought it was entirely possible to have the wrong man strapped to the gurney.

But I didn't say any of that. The professor didn't ask.

Tim walked to the front and told the group he was the assistant warden. He talked for a few minutes about the layout of the Walls. About the upper and lower yards. The hospital. The pickets. I knew they had all craned their necks to stare up at the officers with their shotguns in the pickets on their way in. Visitors always did. He told them about some of the places they'd see in a few minutes. And about some of the places they wouldn't.

"Will we get to see death row?" a tall kid in the back asked. He produced a silly grin, and looked at his classmates.

I looked at him. Maybe I smiled. *Ah, there he is,* I thought. There was always at least one, whatever the group. So this would be the one, this afternoon, to deliver the smartass remarks and be the star. No budding criminologist here, I'd wager. He winked at a pretty girl sitting close to him.

"Death row is not on this unit," Tim told him. "It hasn't been in years. It was on the Ellis Unit for a long time, and has just recently been moved to the Terrell Unit near Livingston. Inmates are transported here on the afternoon of their execution."

The kid looked disappointed; he'd probably had visions of gazing through bars at a group of condemned men, like watching monkeys in a zoo.

"Warden Willett, the senior warden, will take you into the death house," Tim told them, "where you'll see the old death row, as well as the execution chamber."

In my spiel, I gave a short history of the unit. When it was built. Its various additions and renovations. A little about the 1934 breakout. The 1974 Carrasco siege. Most of them listened. A couple asked questions. The tall kid fidgeted, looked at the pretty girl, looked at the door. He was ready to get on with it.

"Warden Willett was a guard in these walls during the Carrasco siege," the professor said. A few of them smiled at me, no doubt in awe of my great age rather than my participation, though slight, in what they must have seen as ancient history.

"Did you get shot?" the tall boy asked, refocused for a least a few seconds.

He appeared disappointed when I said I had not been.

"Did anybody get shot?" he wanted to know.

"People were killed," I told him. "As I believed I mentioned just a few minutes ago."

We led them down the stairs and past the bull ring, where several inmates were laid in, waiting on the bench, probably to see me, probably planning to ask for something they wouldn't get. The kids looked at the men as we passed. We moved by my office, through the long visitation room — empty on a weekday — and out the back, through two chain-link gates, to the death house.

The building itself wasn't likely to impress anybody. Built of the same red bricks as everything else in the Walls, it was tucked in the northeast corner, directly under picket number one. We stopped at the door, and I showed them where the van pulled up to deliver the inmate on his last afternoon. I told them the building had been constructed in 1953, and that it housed the electric chair until the Texas legislature mandated that lethal injection would be the method of execution.

The tall kid, right on cue, stage-whispered "Old Sparky," then sent a hissing sound through his teeth.

We had to crowd into the narrow walkway in the cellblock. I stood by the seventh cell, the next-to-last one at the end. I said that this was the cell in which the inmate spent his final hours. They looked at the slim bunk bolted to the wall, and at the low toilet. I talked them through the procedures. The visit with the chaplain. The phone calls. The last meal.

One student wanted to know the weirdest thing anybody had ever asked for.

"Two boxes of Frosted Flakes. Another one wanted just a jar of dill pickles." I didn't have to rack my memory; every group asked this. "Scotch eggs with syrup. By far the most common last meal is a cheeseburger with fries."

One huge kid — a football player by the looks of him — smiled and nodded his head. A burger and fries didn't seem the worst way to make an exit.

As we moved to the green door of the execution chamber, the class grew louder and more restless. I could hear the tall boy back there, cracking wise about fat convicts giving up their diet for the last meal. He laughed louder than the others. The group was still mumbling when I unlocked the door.

The door swung open. They saw the gurney and fell silent.

Nobody said a word as we crowded around it. Nobody touched it. The students in the back were pressed against the windows of the witness room.

"It's smaller than I expected," one of the girls said.

I didn't know whether she was referring to the gurney or the room. Maybe she meant both. It was a common reaction; people thought executions were big. In reality, the procedure didn't require much space.

I told them about the tie-down team, the medical team, the witnesses, the last statement, the administration of the three drugs. The pronouncement of death. The removal of the body. Then I asked for questions.

They always had questions. The tall kid didn't ask any. He was quieter now, and stared hard at the gurney. I suspected he'd be quieter on the return trip than he had been on the way down here.

Then, like clockwork, one of them maneuvered us into the territory these groups always visited. "Some people," he said, looking at his professor, "think the death penalty is the act of a barbaric society." He looked back at me. "What do you think?"

I paused long enough to make it seem that I was thinking all of this through for the first time.

"When I give the order," I said, "in this room, to cause a person in that room" — I pointed behind me, toward the executioner's area — "to set a process into motion that will result in an inmate's death, I am carrying out the precise order of a court. Which is one of my jobs as the warden of this unit. The decision to kill the inmate was not mine, and was never mine to make. Any more than it was the decision of the executioner who starts the drugs, or the medical technician who inserts the needle, or the tie-down team that secures the inmate. The decision to take this particular life rested wholly with the jury that convicted and sentenced him."

They listened closely, most of their eyes on the gurney's white sheet.

"Now," I went on, still trying to make it seem that this was the first time I'd ever told this to anyone, "the chances are good that none of you will ever have to do what I do, in this room. But you may very well have to serve on a jury in a criminal trial, which means you, yourself, may vote to send someone in here to be executed."

Now some of the eyes widened somewhat.

JIM WILLETT WITH A TOUR GROUP IN THE EXECUTION CHAMBER

JIM WILLETT IN THE EXECUTION CHAMBER

"And if you do, then *you*" — two of them jumped at that — "will be the one causing the deed to be done, not me, or whatever warden stands here and gives the order."

I stole a glance at the professor. He looked unhappy.

Tim conducted the rest of the tour. I followed in case anybody wanted to ask me a question. We took them through the old East Building; one student said it looked like prisons in old movies. Tim said that it had been the prison in several. Hollywood location crews had filmed inside the Walls a few times. We led them beside the upper yard, where inmates paid very little attention to them. The inmates were used to tour groups, used to being stared at.

The three o'clock whistle blew, loud and shrill enough to make some of the students flinch. Tim told them that one blast meant the afternoon count was commencing. When they heard two more, it would mean that every inmate in the unit had been accounted for.

We pointed out the concrete ramp up to the education building where the hostages and their captors had been killed. Then we moved through the tunnel-like passageway between the Four and Five buildings, and into the lower yard. Interest had waned. Visitors who had seen cellblocks straight out of the movies, scenes of hostage-taking and shoot-outs, and the busiest death house in the free world weren't likely to be impressed by workplaces.

We showed them anyway. The mechanical department, we explained, fixes all the non-diesel vehicles in the entire prison system. It's the biggest shop in the lower yard, having taken over space from the shoe shop and license-plate operation; both of those moved to other units. I showed them the media center, and the TV repair shop, and the textile mill that has made cotton into cloth since 1856. This was the stuff I was proudest of, but I didn't expect them to look interested. A prison, at its best, lacks drama.

Tim and I looked at our watches and then at each other. The clear count whistles were overdue. I told the group goodbye, shook the professor's hand, and left my assistant warden to get the class back to their bus. I made my way back through the upper yard to the searcher's desk, where count totals were called in by cellblock officers and department heads.

"What's the problem?" I asked.

An officer put his hand over the mouthpiece of the phone he had been talking into.

"Not clearing yet, Warden."

My next stop was the count room, located directly under the chapel, next to the classification committee room.

The ladies in there were busy double-checking small key-ring tags hanging on hundreds of cup hooks against the paperwork that detailed which inmates had arrived and which had departed the unit since noon. Each rectangular tag represented one prisoner; each was color-coded according to his race. And the two whistles indicating a clear count wouldn't sound until these ladies had exactly the correct tags on exactly the correct hooks. Information was streaming in from the searcher's desk and the various cellblocks. The room was full of people whose chatter did battle with the sound of ringing telephones and the clunk of receivers being dropped into cradles.

Getting a clear count was significantly more difficult at the Walls than at any other prison in Texas. Because of our large, constantly changing transient population, the numbers changed daily, hourly, and sometimes even from minute to minute. It wasn't uncommon for two hundred or more inmates to arrive on a single day, and for that many more to leave on buses headed to other units. Add to that another hundred or so who every weekday walked out the front door with fifty dollars of taxpayers' money and a voucher for a bus ticket if they needed one. Then there were the roughly thirteen hundred permanent inmates. Knowing where everybody was at any one moment was one hell of a job.

But we did it. At least nine times a day, every day. Three hundred and sixty-five days a year. And sometimes more often than that if, for instance, someone spotted a person near the unit, off state property, dressed completely in white.

Anyone who had lived in Huntsville for any length of time knew that it wasn't the best of ideas, ever, to dress completely in white.

A FEW MINUTES BEFORE FOUR O'CLOCK, CAPTAIN TERRY GREEN STEPPED INTO MY office and told me they'd tried twice and couldn't get a clear count.

He stared at me, not having to ask his question.

"Rack 'em up," I said.

Now the situation grew more serious. Now each and every inmate would be sent to his cell and locked up until the numbers cleared. The workday would be halted in the lower yard, and all those inmates brought back to their blocks. They'd all have to be strip-searched, every mother's son of them, as they always were when they moved from shop to living areas. Other operations, like the next count, would fall behind schedule, and the evening meal would be delayed. The grievance officer's mailbox would be full for days.

I went back to the searcher's desk and waited for Terry to bring me good news. Which he finally did.

I was at my own desk when the two whistles sang out, the most beautiful sound a warden can hear inside a prison. I leaned back in my chair and could almost feel the unit return to normal. Like a massive living thing, veins and arteries flowing. Muscles stretching. Cell doors sliding open and hundreds of men moving at once. It was a good feeling.

Not clearing count was one of the bad possibilities, topped only by breakouts, sieges and riots. Not clearing count, at its simplest level, meant that somebody — at least one somebody — might be out. And our job — our single, abiding function — was to insure that inmates stayed in.

The office was quiet after the two whistles. It was time for me to go home. But the papers on my desk told me that I wouldn't for a while yet. I got Kim on the intercom and told her to call the searchers' desk and find out if the inmates who had been laid in because they had requested to see were still in the bull ring or if they had been sent back to their cells.

In a minute, she called to tell me they were still outside, waiting.

The first was an old man who said he just couldn't get along with his cellie.

"I tried and tried, Warden," he said, standing in front of my desk, "and I even prayed at it. But we just don't gee and haw, the two of us. I was raised on a farm. I was a farmer till I come here."

I looked down at the file Kim had brought me. Apparently, somewhere along the way, grand theft had replaced horticulture. He'd been in and out for decades, and had made the grand tour of units all over the state.

"Dinkins" — that was his cellmate — "he's from downtown Houston. The bad part. He don't know a single thing about farming, nor care about it neither. So we don't have nothing to talk about."

He was quiet for a moment.

"We near come to fisticuffs the other night, Warden. And I don't want to lose my good time."

I told him I'd check into the matter and scribbled a note to talk to the major. The inmate would almost certainly be moved to another cell.

Next came a young fellow of twenty-five or so. His story was that he and his ex-wife were trying to patch things up and he wanted to be allowed a contact visit. Before Ruiz vs. Estelle, there hadn't been any such thing; all inmates had done their visiting on weekends through wire mesh and glass at the long tables in the visitation room. Now we had a freestanding building in the old rodeo arena, where some inmates could hug and hold on to their wives and their children for a few minutes. It wasn't as much contact as they'd like, but it was certainly better than they'd had before Ruiz.

I granted his request. With prisoners' requests, as with employee discipline, I usually opted for the most lenient decisions that seemed reasonable. The two most precious things that inmates had were family visits and commissary privileges. If I took those away, a man didn't have a lot to lose in prison. And that made him dangerous.

The next guy wanted a job change. He worked in the laundry, and he must have figured that, since it was already hot there in spring, it would be broiling by summer. I told him to see the major. He was the one I designated to reassign jobs, and I made it a policy to stay out of his business.

The last inmate complained that his radio had been confiscated. I looked at his name on the I-60, then told him I would check into it. I didn't mention that his mother had called.

Now they were all gone. So were the secretaries, the clerks, and the porter. The daylight was muted, giving itself over to dusk. I stood up, stretched, and looked at the papers on my desk that would have to be dealt with in the morning. I put on my jacket and turned off the light.

Pollis, the night records clerk, was already at one of the desks in the outer office. He was a student at Sam Houston, majoring in computer programming. Pollis was a good kid, and a good employee. On many afternoons, when I was on my way out, we chatted a few minutes about computers. It was a good transition for me, from on duty to off. Though I'd learned long ago that wardens are never really off duty.

Pollis and I didn't chat that evening. I was too tired.

In the hall, I nodded at some of the officers coming off their pickets to eat supper, told the radio picket officer I was going home, and stepped into an evening dominated by a vast, red-streaked sky.

I walked my hundred yards more slowly than I had that morning, and inside the house, had a few minutes to look at the Huntsville Item while Janice finished up in the kitchen. Then we sat down to our dinner with Jordan, who had a story or two about school that day. Janice said that Jacob had called from college. It was baseball season, and his news was all about that. Then Janice said something about something that happened at work.

I listened. But I was thinking about that young officer in his picket. I hoped he'd stay awake, and that he wouldn't turn up in front of my desk again.

I was thinking, too, about the old barber, and hoping that his pain in his feet and legs would subside enough for him to get some sleep in his cell. And that he'd make his parole, and finally get to go fishing.

I was thinking about that family I'd met at Peckerwood Hill. Of the old woman and her hymn. Of the son and brother that they left there under the tall pines, who surely didn't turn out how — or end up where — they would have wished.

And I was thinking of that other little family. Still on the long road back to Amarillo, without the boy they had come for, with no money for a motel or a good meal. I hoped they could keep enough water in their old truck to get them all the way home.

EXECUTION JOURNAL

Number seventy-two
June 21-22, 2000

Gary Graham, death row inmate no. 696, arrives at the death house at 6:30 p.m. after a short journey from the Terrell Unit. It's a pretty drive, through a part of Texas known as the Big Thicket, dense woodlands overflowing with majestic pines. It's a peaceful place. But Graham shows up in anything but a peaceful mood.

He's long proclaimed his innocence to anyone who will listen — and many prominent people have. He was convicted in 1981 for robbing and murdering a man in the parking lot of a Safeway supermarket in Houston. As his date with the gurney has drawn nearer, several celebrities have spoken out against his execution. Danny Glover, the actor, has been particularly vocal. As his witnesses for tomorrow, Graham has listed Reverend Jesse Jackson, Al Sharpton, Bianca Jagger, and "George Bush, Jr.," whom he identifies as a "frnd."

He's lying in the floor of the van when we open the back doors. His leg irons and handcuffs are attached to a belly chain. He's thirty-nine years old, black, two inches shy of six feet tall. He weighs about a hundred and fifty pounds and might just be the angriest person I've ever seen. There's nothing in his eyes but pure hatred. His body is tense. Rigid. Like a cornered animal.

His execution isn't scheduled until tomorrow evening, almost a full twenty-four hours away. Because of the intense media coverage, we're breaking a long-established precedent of not moving a condemned inmate into the death house until the afternoon of the procedure. By moving him early and unannounced, we hoped to avoid a convoy of television and radio helicopters and vehicles trailing along. What we didn't need was a parade leading up to tomorrow's spectacle. Also, there is always the chance of protesters — for and against — lining the highway. There will be plenty of that outside the Walls soon enough. Usually the groups are quiet, and mostly respectful, of the event and each other. But we're well aware that tomorrow the range will be a wide one: everything from the Ku Klux Klan to an outfit calling itself the New Black Panthers, which has stated its intention to march in full military gear, carrying rifles.

Major Dean approaches the van and lays out the situation clearly for Graham: "You can step out and walk inside, or you will be carried."

Graham doesn't look at the major. Doesn't respond.

I point at a group of officers already in riot gear. They get in the van and carry him, holding his shoulders and legs, into the death house, placing him in the third cell in the row of eight. This, too, is different from standard operating procedure. We've been using the seventh cell,

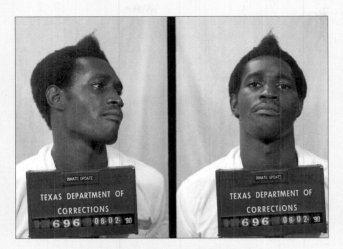

GARY GRAHAM, DEATH ROW INMATE NO. 696

but in preparation for this particular inmate, I had the bunk taken out of this cell and a stool bolted in place. The old porcelain sink and toilet have also been replaced with a stainless-steel combination unit. Porcelain breaks into sharp-edged shards. I chose the third cell for these renovations because it is closer to the execution chamber, giving Graham less time to do the kicking and screaming that he's publicly vowed to do as he's carried to the gurney.

Inside the cell, he resists the officers without actually fighting them. In his current condition, a fight would be hard to wage: The leg irons and cuffs are attached to the belly shackle by a chain short enough to keep him from standing fully erect. The officers remove all of the restraints and all of his clothes. Now they hold him down — unshackled, he poses more of a danger — while Sergeant Dickey steps in to fingerprint him. When he's finished, the team backs out of the cell, one at a time.

Graham gets up off the floor and steps up to the bars. He's moving something in his mouth — maybe saliva that he intends to spit at one of us, or maybe something else. He holds his head up higher, stretching upward to such an extent that the muscles in his neck and chest tighten. Everyone backs away.

Major Dean holds up a pair of paper overalls. "These are for you to put on," he tells Graham. "Now open your mouth so I can see inside."

Graham explodes into a tirade that concludes with specific instructions regarding what the major and the rest of us could do to ourselves.

Finally, maybe because he realizes that he'll have to stand there naked until he does what he's been told, he opens his mouth, but only halfway.

Major Dean isn't satisfied, but the regional director, who probably wants to just get on with it, tells him to hand him the overalls. Graham puts them on.

Everyone not assigned to the Walls leaves the room. I tell my people that I don't want anyone getting close to this man. If they have to approach the bars, then Graham is to move to the very back of the cell. I tell them that under no circumstances is an officer to open the cell door without the entire team being present.

"I don't care if he has a razor blade in his mouth," I tell them. "If he cuts himself up, then you let him lay right there and bleed until the rest of the team gets here."

I ask if they understand. They each tell me they do.

I go to my office, leaving two sergeants and Chaplain Brazzil with the man who will be on front pages around the world tomorrow or the next day. Around 7:30, I walk back to give the inmate my typical summary of what will take place tomorrow.

"I'll come to get you tomorrow evening at six," I tell him. "If you don't follow me voluntarily, then I will have officers remove you from your cell and carry you into the next room."

"I understand that," he says. He's standing in the middle of the cell, in his paper overalls. He wears the same livid scowl he did earlier.

"By the way," I tell him, just before I leave to go home, "you are the first person to spend the night in this cellblock in thirty-four years."

He squints his angry eyes, and gives me a look that leaves no doubt how he feels about that honor.

I get to my office before daylight on what I know will be one hell of a long day. There are thirty or so media trucks and vans parked on the northwest side of the Walls, with more probably on the way. I convinced Janice to take half the day off and to take Jordan to her mother's house out in the country till tomorrow.

The volatile gathering promises trouble. Today I expect legions both in favor of the death penalty and opposed to it; racially motivated fringe groups that detest each other; and a virtual army of official forces — the prison system's internal affairs unit, local EMS, the Huntsville police department, the Walker County sheriff's department, Texas Highway Patrol troopers, Texas Rangers, and the FBI.

There will even be a state helicopter whopping overhead, no doubt along with others carrying TV reporters. Bianca Jagger will be here, and Jesse Jackson will bring an entourage. Quanell X, a radical Muslim leader, plans to show up.

And all of the hoopla will play out at my unit. It's been just a week since I was given the most prestigious award in the prison system: Warden of the Year. Now I'd better prove I deserved it.

To the pair of sergeants who will be in the death house from six until ten, I give the same instructions that I gave last night: Graham is to be treated with extreme caution. Throughout the day, he receives visits from a few family members and supporters.

Midmorning, Tim New and I attend a meeting in the contact visiting room, out in the old rodeo arena. The regional director told all the other wardens in his charge to be on hand today, along with more than a hundred members of their uniformed supervisory staff. This meeting is to assign specific duties. Barricades are set up around the unit, and each section will have to be manned. All streets within a block of the Walls are closed to traffic. The director says a specific concern is the New Black Panthers, a Dallas group that says it intends to use assault rifles (supposedly unloaded) as part of their marching drill. It's against the law to bring weapons — unloaded or not — on prison property. As for areas outside the unit, we have a brand-new law on our side, which makes it illegal to bring firearms within a thousand feet of a school. The third floor of the education building is a school — part of the prison system's Windham ISD, the largest school district in Texas.

The media is spread over the west lawn of the old administration building, which places them directly between the protesters on the west side who oppose capital punishment, and those on the east side who favor it.

Talk about being in the crossfire.

███

By midafternoon everyone, official and unofficial, is in place for whatever this turns out to be. At one point the Dallas group, without rifles, makes its way around the front of the old administration building, obviously headed for a confrontation with the Ku Klux Klan. But a particularly ominous-looking riot team of Texas Rangers quicksteps single-file toward them, and the New Black Panthers reconsider their plan and go back to where they were.

Number seventy-two
June 21-22, 2000

The place is boiling with emotion. Spontaneous speeches erupt. One woman calls for the death of the executioner. Governor George Bush is denounced frequently. There is singing. Some chanting. More than a little yelling. Bottles get tossed. People get arrested. An American flag gets burned.

Larry Fitzgerald, the public information officer, tells the media that the state parole board has unanimously decided to not interfere with the execution. The news spreads outward like wildfire into both camps. And the intensity, if possible, grows.

I stand on the front porch for a while and watch as Jesse Jackson shouts out an angry speech that loses much of its effectiveness in the thunderous hullabaloo. Jackson, undeterred, soldiers on.

Almost a hundred miles to the north, my mother is watching all of this on CNN. She sees me on the front porch, calls our house, gets no answer, and calls Janice's mother's house. She tells Janice to call the prison and tell somebody to make me go inside.

It looks to her like I'm standing in a dangerous place.

———

Last-minute legal maneuvers cause us to stand near telephones until a little after seven, when we learn that all

MAJOR DEAN WITH THE CELL EXTRACTION TEAM

of Gary Graham's streams of appeal have run dry.

My team is suited in riot gear and ready to go. We all walk back to the death house and the team and I go into the cellblock. Graham is standing at the rear of the cell.

"It's time to come with me now," I tell him. "I need you to move up to the bars and put your hands though the slot so we can handcuff you."

He shakes his head. He tells me he's not coming.

"Then we're going to come in and get you."

His eyes go narrow now. His fists clench. Though he is in the paper coveralls, I can tell that his entire body is clenching.

"Come on," he breathes.

An officer unlocks the door. Major Dean, shield in hand, charges in. Graham kicks the shield, but the major pins him to the floor as the other five officers rush in. They soon have the inmate in restraints.

I am the first into the execution chamber, with Chaplain Brazzil right behind me. We watch the team carry Graham in, his entire body convulsing. They thrust him onto the gurney. Major Dean holds his head down so he can't spit on anyone. Finally he is handcuffed to the gurney, and his head, midsection, and legs are strapped down tightly. Each member of the team is breathing loudly. During the struggle, one leg of the paper coveralls was ripped all the way up to the crotch. I call out to the cellblock for somebody to bring me a sheet, and the chaplain places it over Graham's lower body before the witnesses are led into the two galleries.

I dismiss the move team and call in the medical team. They quickly locate good veins in each arm, insert the IVs, and leave.

Now it's just Graham, Brazzil, and me. Often this is when an inmate confides. Cries. Confesses.

Not tonight, I'm thinking.

The witnesses move into place on the other side of the window. Janie Cockrell, the deputy director of the Texas prison system, steps to the door and says I can proceed. I tell Graham he may make a statement now, if he wishes.

He begins by saying that he never killed anybody, then speeds up and shouts that we need to stop killing black people. He goes on for five minutes, which is the time limit I gave him last night. He finally stops, and I ask if he's done. He starts again, delivering at breakneck speed a long harangue about racial prejudice and injustice. After nearly six more minutes, I sigh, lift my glasses from the bridge of my nose, and watch, about thirty seconds later, as Graham falls asleep in mid-sentence.

The witnesses are led out. The IVs are removed. The funeral home people take the body.

Wayne Scott, the director of the prison system asks if I'm okay. We go way back, Wayne and I. He hired on as a new boot at the Walls just a few months after I did. He knows this has been a particularly hard one for me. Wayne knows that they are all hard for me. He shakes my hand and gives me a half-hug with his other arm, then turns to go.

"By the way," he says, "I like the sheet."

Tomorrow, I'll tell Chaplain Brazzil that from now on we'll use the sheet.

Outside the circus continues. The reporters who witnessed the procedure each make statements at the podium in front of the unit. Each takes questions. Then the inmate's witnesses do the same, though their comments are more caustic, more venomous. Each takes a long time in the spotlights, Jesse Jackson an extremely long time.

I know they believe what they're saying. And I agree that, over the years, innocent people, of all races, may have been put to death. The sheer number of executions — by rope, electric chair, and needle — indicate that this might be the case. But why people like Jackson and Jagger chose to champion an obvious hoodlum like Graham bewilders me.

Slowly, the crowd dissolves. The big clock on the front of the unit says it's a little after ten. It's been over fifteen hours since I climbed out of bed, and it feels like it.

I drop heavily down to the edge of a brick flower bed and sit awhile. Lepher Jenkins, my regional director, sits beside me, just as exhausted. We don't talk; we just sit. We'll be here until the area is completely clear, and that won't be until Jesse Jackson and Bianca Jagger are through giving interviews.

The television lights shut down one by one, returning more of the grass to the summer night. People get into vehicles and drive away, and soon not many are left. Lepher and I look at the emptying place that is not at all unlike it was all those years ago, on another summer night, after the Carrasco siege.

We're too tired to talk about it. So we just sit. And watch Reverend Jesse Jackson go on. And on. And on.

EPILOGUE

OLD SPARKY, THE MOST POPULAR ATTRACTION IN
Texas Prison Museum, never seemed as intimida
in its display setting as it had when I used to ta
squad of convicts into the death house to clean. It
been in its natural element back then, in the pl
where it had done its gruesome work, in that c
little room, always either too hot or too cold, wh
inmates felt the presence of ghosts. Here, beh
three glass walls and in front of a panel of fake
bricks, it never made me think of an arrogant l
full of its prey. Now it looked more like a trophy
taxidermist's collection.

It was the first thing visitors wanted to see a
they paid their admission. I thought the impres
scale model of the Walls, under its Plexiglas do
covering a space the size of a ping-pong table, oug
draw their attention. It had been carefully assemb
piece by piece, by an inmate. Since coming on part-
at the museum after my retirement from the pr
system, I'd studied that model closely, looking
mistakes. I only found a couple, and they were mi
It was an impressive thing, that model, but m
folks sailed right past it, their sonar locked on v
they had come to see.

When construction was finished on the new, big
museum out by the Interstate, Old Sparky and the
model and all the other exhibits would move to

new digs. Along with one old warden, I supposed, who could answer visitors' questions and point out a thing or two on the model of the aged fortress that stood just up the hill.

From my counter, I watched a young fellow make his way down that hill. Anybody in town could have told you what he was up to. Huntsville folk had spent their whole lives watching men step back out into the world.

The white bag he carried would have been enough to give him away, but his shirt was the clincher. The prison system could send them out in some real doozies. This one was a couple of sizes too big for his slender frame, as long as a nightshirt, and a bright, splashy pink.

He stopped in front of the museum, read the sign carefully, and came in.

"I just now got released," he told me at the counter. I tried to look as if it was news to me.

"That's good. Congratulations."

"My dad's coming to get me." He looked over at the big model. "He said the only place he knew about was this museum, and for me to meet him here. Will that be all right?"

"That'll be fine."

He looked at the model again, then at the little sign that gave the admission price. He gave me two of the fifty dollars he had been issued.

"Do you think I could put my bag down back there with you?" he asked.

I put it under the counter. Give or take a few items, I knew what was in it. A radio. A fan. A comb. A packet of letters. Some photographs from home. His parole paperwork. Maybe a couple of paperback novels.

He was over at the big model now.

"I come out right there." He pressed a fingertip on the Plexiglas directly over the front porch. He moved along a few steps. "Spent the night in yonder." Now the finger hovered over the transient block.

A family came in. The father paid me. He asked where Old Sparky was, and off they went.

In a few minutes, the young man was back at the counter.

"I got a little while to wait yet," he told me. "Any place around here where

I can get something to eat?" It was mid-afternoon. After years of being marched into three squares a day, he must only now have realized that providing his lunch was now his own affair.

I told him that if he was in the mood for a chicken-fried steak, The Texan Café was his best bet. I pointed out the window to its corner.

"And they make a good sandwich over at King's Candies." I told him where it was on the other side of the square.

The family had left, and I was standing outside on the sidewalk when he came back. He hadn't been gone long enough to have eaten.

"Couldn't you find anything?" I asked.

He nodded, and sat on the curb.

"I went to the sandwich place," he said. He rested his arms on his knees.

"They was some girls in there. Eating. They went to giggling when they saw me." He kicked softly at a pebble. "I guess I sort of lost my appetite."

I sat down beside him. I told him there would be some of that.

He nodded. Over the next few minutes he told me about his dad, who had raised him by himself. And a little about prison life. He'd been locked up for eleven years, but not all in one stretch. He'd done time at Pack II the year before I had gone there as assistant warden, but I didn't tell him that. I just listened. He'd gotten into a fight or two there and had been transferred to Coffield. Then to some other places. His last stretch had been at the Allred Unit, near Wichita Falls.

"I had to quit smoking while I was in," he told me. "And that's good. I don't intend to go back to that."

He got quiet then. We watched the traffic on the square.

"It was drugs that got me in trouble in the first place," he finally said, as directly as if I had asked. "I truly hope I can stay clear of them now."

A few afternoon clouds had moved in. Somebody waved at me from a car.

"You need to make sure you do that," I said. "If you have to go back in, you'll likely be an old man before you get out next time."

He nodded. He'd seen plenty of old men.

I asked if he had a trade.

"I do." He smiled. "I'm a welder. That's one thing I learned in there. That, and how to quit smoking."

I was back inside the museum when he came in to get his bag.

"He's here," he told me.

I watched through the window as he stepped down off the sidewalk to wait for the pickup to pull to a stop. He held the big bag in one hand and attempted to wave with the other.

A man in his sixties got out of the truck. They shook hands. Stiffly. Awkwardly. Obviously not knowing quite how to go about this. Then the older man put his hand on his son's shoulder, and the boy dissolved into his open arms. Into a long, tight, who-gives-a-damn-that-we're-on-a-busy-street bear hug. When they were done, they said a few things to each other, got in the truck, and drove away.

I went out on the sidewalk and watched the pickup until it was out of sight.

Up the hill, a sharp whistle announced the three o'clock count was commencing in the Walls. I looked at my watch. Right on time.

I stood there until two more whistles sang out that the count was clear.

UPDATE

Major Dick Andrews retired from the Ferguson Unit in 1984.

Dr. Geoge Beto left his job as the prison director in 1972 and became a professor of criminology and corrections at Huntsville's Sam Houston State University. The university's Criminal Justice Center, constructed by inmates, is named after him. A prison unit is also named in his honor.

Officer Black left the prison system after finishing college and I've not seen him since. I never knew his first name.

Sergeant Elzie Black retired from the Walls Unit in 1977.

Chaplain Jim Brazzil witnessed 157 executions before becoming a member of the prison system's Victim Services team. As a part of this job he continues to witness executions.

Inmate James Brewer was paroled in 1975. He returned as a parole violator three days before Christmas 1989 and died twelve days later.

Eroy Brown was acquitted of the murders of Warden Wallace Pack and Farm Manager Billy Moore. Brown was paroled. He is currently serving a ninety-year sentence in a federal penitentiary.

S. B. Cauthen retired from the Walls as a lieutenant in 1976.

Officer Frank Chance retired in 1976.

Janie Cockrell retired in 2003.

Kenneth Coleman retired as a parole board member in 1993.

Inmate Ignacio Cuevas was executed at the Walls Unit in 1991.

Major Kenneth Dean is now an assistant warden at the Wynne Unit.

Sergeant Grant Dickey now works as an assistant to Tim New.

Warden Ron Drewry retired in 1998.

Director W. J. Estelle retired in 1983. There is a prison unit near Huntsville named for him.

Larry Fitzgerald retired in 2004.

John Gilbert currently serves as the deputy director of private facilities for the Correctional Institutions Division of the Texas Department of Criminal Justice.

Captain Terry Green retired in 2002.

Dianne Guillory remains as the human resources supervisor at the Walls Unit.

Inmate Lawrence Hall died in 1993.

Warden Lawrence Harvey was promoted to the director of the prison system's training department and retired in that capacity in 1993.

Officer Bobby Heard left the prison system in 1977 for a different line of work.

Aline House retired from the Windham School District in 1977.

Warden H. H. Husbands retired in 1978.

Lepher Jenkins retired in 2000.

Glenn Johnson retired from the prison system's Windham School District in 1986.

Captain John Lindsey became an assistant warden, then retired in 1994.

Bobby Maggard retired as the warden of the Pack II Unit in 1985.

D. V. "Red" McKaskle retired as interim director of the Texas Department of Corrections in November 1984 and has been the chief deputy at the Harris County Sheriff's Office for many years.

Major A. J. Murdock died suddenly from a stroke in 1982.

Tim New was promoted to warden at another unit the day I retired. He is now the assistant director of security systems for the Texas Department of Criminal Justice–Correctional Institutions Division.

Bruce Noviskie was promoted to education consultant at another prison unit and left the system in 1979 to pursue another career.

Father Joseph O'Brien remained at the Walls Unit as the Catholic chaplain until 1981, when he left the prison system and moved to a parish in South Texas.

Jerry Peterson retired in 1997 as deputy director for operations at the Texas Department of Criminal Justice–Institutional Division.

Officer David Pollis still works the night shift in the warden's office.

Keith Price retired as a warden in 2003

Captain Hugh Pritchett rose to the rank of assistant warden and retired in 1984.

Jack Pursley retired as warden of the Walls Unit in 1993.

Kent Ramsey retired in 1999 as assistant director of Region 1 for the Texas Department of Criminal Justice–Institutional Division. He and I remain good friends.

Inmate Steve Roach was released on parole in 1977 but returned on a parole violation in 1982. He was paroled again in 2001.

Wayne Scott became the director of the Texas Department of Criminal Justice and retired in 2001. There is a prison unit named after him.

Inmate Kenneth Stafford was paroled in 1999. He returned to Huntsville that December to deliver a Christmas present to Jordan and died a few weeks later.

Charlie Strban, the man inside the pill window in Chapter 3, later became a hospital administrator and eventually was promoted to assistant warden and served as my only assistant warden during my years at the Diagnostic Unit. Charlie became ill shortly before I moved to the Walls Unit. He retired in 1999 and died shortly thereafter.

Bruce Thaler rose through the ranks and was honored as warden of the year in 1997. He retired in 2002.

Ed Trainor joined the Air Force not long after his part in the story. He came to Huntsville and visited with me in 1980. I've not heard from him since.

Inmate Donald Walker was paroled in 1994. He returned as a parole violator the following year and was paroled again in 2002.

My mother, Louise Willett, is alive and well and still living in Groesbeck.

Linda Woodman became a warden. She retired in 1985, and a prison unit in Gatesville is named after her.

Doors and pickets were added to the sides of the Education Department at the Walls Unit. No more hostage situations have occurred. In 1998 the Education Building was named the Standley-Beseda Education Department in honor of the two women who died there in 1974.

The last Texas Prison Rodeo took place in 1986. The Texas Department of Corrections declared that the stadium was unsafe, and that it couldn't afford the repairs.

The old barber in Chapter 16 was paroled in February 2002. He called to let me know that he went fishing.

PHOTO CREDITS

Dickenson, J. D.; 192-193

Landry, Burke; 123

Lichtenstein, Andrew; 2-3 courtesy Aurora Photo, 204

Moore, Bruce, TDCJ Media Services; 4, 200, 203, 211

Nira, Richard; 12-13, 181

TDCJ Media Services; 6-7, 27, 35, 37, 38, 43, 50, 55, 58, 64, 66, 69, 78-79, 94-95, 107, 109, 110, 112, 115, 124, 125, 126, 127, 128-129, 130, 161, 164, 170, 173, 175, 178, 186, 214

Texas Prison Museum 136, 139, 211

Wall, Keith, TDCJ Media Services; 48

Willett, Janice; 23, 157, 168

Willett, Jim; 77, 158, 189, 191, 221

A FEW LAST WORDS ON PRISONS

As bad as we are failing as a society — considering all the people we have locked up, we must be failing — we owe it to ourselves and our prisoners to provide them opportunities to lead productive lives when released back into the free world.

Three essential tools to bring this about are:

- Classroom education. A sound and useful academic curriculum should continue to be offered, so that inmates can acquire the knowledge, as well as the degrees and certifications, required to compete in the job market.

- Vocational training. Those inmates who don't choose the academic route should be given the opportunity to learn a specific trade. Inmates who are turned back into the world without a means of supporting themselves and being a productive citizen stand a staggeringly high chance of returning to prison.

- Morality-based (or faith-based) programs. The simple truth is that a majority of inmates are incarcerated because they lacked the moral compass necessary to make wise, positive plans and carry them out. These programs have very good success rates in this regard. But programs like this won't work magic; it is impossible to correct in prison all the wrongs of poor parenting or society's ills. Our prisons wouldn't be nearly as full as they are, nor would we need so many of them, if we all revisited the basic thou shalt nots of the Ten Commandments.

For rehabilitation to have any chance of success, the inmate must desire to improve himself.

Regarding the actual time spent in prison, I believe we have gotten much too soft on convicts. I would never advocate anything cruel, but I believe inmates should be made to work hard enough so that prison itself should be a reason not to want to return. They should be punished when they refuse to work, and solitary confinement should go back to being what it used to be: bread and water for most meals, a solid door closed most of the time, with only motivational reading at hand, for up to fifteen days at a time. To those who think this too extreme, I would say this: Every old convict I've talked to says that the old-style solitary confinement, administered fairly and humanely, was far more effective as a deterrent than the new kind, in which an inmate retains most of the usual prison amenities. There is much to be said for reaping what you sow. And there is nothing at all wrong with hard work. Such measures during incarceration, along with academic, vocational, and moral training, will lower the rate of recidivism as well as the cost to taxpayers.

ACKNOWLEDGMENTS

This book would not have been possible without the help of Nancye Gardner; Judy Mancil; and Jene Robbins.

Thanks also go to Carla Christian; Kenneth Coleman; Doug Dretke; Terry Green; Bill Harper; Sean Holtz of Baseball Almanac; Glenn Johnson; Jack King; John Lindsey; Warden Mark Louflin; Bobby Maggard; Mary C. Moore; Avery Patterson; Hugh Pritchett; Jack Pursley; Cindy Reed; Wayne Scott; Kenneth Simmons; Joe Smith; Molly Standley; Teresa Staples; Bruce Thaler; Billy Ware; Wesley Warner; and Larry Westerdauhl.

The authors wish to especially thank our agent Jacques de Spoelberch for his constant faith in this project, our editor Lisa Gray for her tireless work, our designers DJ Stout and Julie Savasky of Pentagram Design for the dramatic presentation, and our publisher Rue Judd for bringing *Warden* to life.

Andrew Lichtenstein's photos have greatly helped us tell our story.

And a very special thank-you goes to Sara Rimer, of the *New York Times*, who first suggested that Jim should write a book.